JANNETTA COLLINS-JOHNSON is a Trinidadian mother, grandmother, friend, confidante, and stand-in-mother to many. The stories and didactic moments she chronicles in this book, form a clear pattern of God's tapestry in her life. She shares those stories and moments and succeeds incredibly well in painting a picture of a God who leads and directs our lives no matter what comes our way.

Acknowledgments for *A Simple Man's Walk*

Jannetta is one of the most amazing women of God that I have had the privilege of knowing. I believe that her walk with God has been so divinely ordered because of her commitment to walk in Agape. There is no other explanation to the end that she would go to reach out to people who are in need. She does it with great joy and very often to her own discomfort, inconvenience and sometimes while being misunderstood by others. It is this God-given ability that has led her to these extra-ordinary moments in her life that she has shared with us so freely in this book that we too can be so divinely inspired and challenged in our own lives.

Over the many years of being her Pastor she has always amazed me by her faithfulness in service to her Lord. The many challenges she faced seem to strengthen her resolve to continue in love and to show to all that Love truly never fails. Many may look for the greats in the pulpits and in corridors of the earthly famous but the many and simple like Jannetta are the ones that will shine brightly in God's eyes. These are the ones who will be known as the greatest for they have embraced the heart of the Father to live by Love which is the greatest of All.

May this book open our eyes to see that there is indeed "a more excellent way"

Pastor Kelvin Siewdass

Pastor of Trinidad Christian Center
Corner Morne Coco and Simeon Roads,
Petit Valley.
Trinidad and Tobago.

For me, nothing brings home a point as much as testimonies of life experiences. In reading "A Simple Man's Walk with God", you will be inspired and encouraged to step out in faith and follow in the Master's footsteps. You will experience His love and compassion, His grace and His mercy, His discipline and His guidance, His strength and His comfort, His peace and His joy. Your life will be changed forever!

Peggy Ng-See-Quan
Elder
Church of Scotland
Trinidad and Tobago

This book, without a doubt, stirs a holy envy and yet, a fiery passion within me to "Go"—

For I was an hungred, and ye gave me meat: I was thirsty, and ye gave me drink: I was a stranger, and ye took me in: 36 Naked, and ye clothed me: I was sick, and ye visited me: I was in prison, and ye came unto me. 37 Then shall the righteous answer him, saying, Lord, when saw we thee an hungred, and fed thee? Or thirsty, and gave thee drink? 38 When saw we thee a stranger, and took thee in? Or naked, and clothed thee? 39 Or when saw we thee sick, or in prison, and came unto thee? 40 And the King shall answer and say unto them, Verily I say unto you, Inasmuch as ye have done it unto one of the least of these my brethren, ye have done it unto me.
—Matthew 25:35-40

What untiring service unto the Lord! What readiness and availability to GO!

This book sizzles with a bold and brave energy that responds to the very breath of our Lord as the author hears His even-silent desire to meet a need—no "passing the buck", but ever present to give of herself in compassion to lift the plight of another.

Truth be told, I fall way short of such unwavering service in His Kingdom. Thankfully, these shared experiences arouse in me a longing to serve. Be assured that they will do the same for you!
In these difficult times when no government has the answer to the predicament of many, the simplicity of her service, as herein expressed, offers hope to me and to you, that we too could be light in this dark world, as we serve our beloved Lord and Saviour with the same level of joy and accomplishment.
Be encouraged as you read!

Althea Bastien- Trinidad Christian Center

I was very impressed that without the usual literary training, the Author would attempt to write this book. She knew that if encouraged, others could receive the same guidance from God which she has experienced in her life. That's great and I am happy that it has come to fruition.
Crossing religious denominations she has reached a wide range of people because of her passion to help others. Out of her desire to touch others whom she could not reach by personal contact she hopes to cross geographical boundaries in order to inspire through the writing of her experiences.
As you go through the pages of "A Simple Man's Walk with God" please pray for humility to seek God's guidance in your own life.

Audrey McDowall, Hanover Methodist Church

To walk with God is to be so passionately in love with Him that consumed by His love your chief delight is to do your simple part to respond to the desire of His heart - that none should perish. Transformed by His love you relentlessly pursue the unlovely, snatching them out of the kingdom of darkness into an eternally life- saving relationship with Jesus; the One Whose love is perfect.

My 'Mummy" Jannetta is one such rescuer...
As one of Jannetta's many spiritual children for close to twenty years, and as one who remembers what it was to be unlovely, I have had the distinct honour of being a direct recipient of her profoundly powerful love; a love, daily fuelled by her amazing intimacy with God. She has taught me how to seek God's face, to pray, to love, to serve and how to be a devoted wife and mother. "The devil is a liar!" Jannetta would often say. Words that have inspired me to keep my eyes on God and to diligently pursue His truth. As a result of the many deposits my modern day "Eunice" and my children's modern day "Lois" has made in our lives, there is no doubt that Jannetta's spiritual legacy will live on through us.

Inspired by her humility and the simplicity of her life surrendered to God, generations of 'simple men' will arise to continue to spoil the devil at every turn during their ordinary lives.

Let "A Simple Man's Walk with God" transform you and cause you to accept the invitation to join the ever growing army of God in this end time revival to take back everything the devil has ever stolen from the Kingdom of God.

Colleen Davis,
Trinidad Christian Center

A SIMPLE MAN'S WALK WITH GOD

JANNETTA
COLLINS-JOHNSON

A SIMPLE MAN'S WALK Copyright © 2016
Layout Design by dArtery
All Rights Reserved
International Copyright Secured
Cover Design by Ryan Drye
Photography by Jonelle Roberts-Porter

Collins-Johnson, Jannetta
A Simple Man's Walk. : DAMGRP, 2016 (Christian).
— ISBN - 978098440165- (paperback)
ISBN - 9780984401666- (ebook)
Religious; Devotional; USA; Trinidad & Tobago

THE DIGITAL ARTERY MEDIA GROUP PUBLISHERS
Tampa, Florida

CONTENTS

Prologue 11

Preface 13

Introduction - My Purpose, My Destiny 19

Chapter 1 - Supernatural Walk 27

Chapter 2 – Grace!!! Guards and Guides 35

Chapter 3 - Faith 41

Chapter 4 - Fear vs. Faith 49

Chapter 5 - God's Purpose Achieved Through Sacrifice 55

Chapter 6 - A Book of Remembrance 61

Chapter 7 - God's Perfect Plan; God Loves Agreement 69

Chapter 8 - Trip to Texas 73

Chapter 9 - Our Expectations vs. God's Plan 77

Chapter 10 - We are God's Workmanship 85

Chapter 11 - Tried and Tested 95

Chapter 12 - Learning Through Experiences 101

Chapter 13 - A Battle Won vs. Winning a Battle 105

Chapter 14 - Visa Time (Book by Chapter) 113

Chapter 15 - Decision Time 117

Chapter 16 - Train Up a Child, and Let Him Go 123

Chapter 17 - Young Kings 133

Chapter 18 - A Grandmother's Joy 139

Chapter 19 - God's Love Bubbles Over 141

Chapter 20 - Becoming Love 145

Chapter 21 - Sharing God's Love 153

Chapter 22 - God's Peace in Worship 157

Chapter 23 - The Touch of a Father 161

Chapter 24 - A Father's Legacy to His Son 165

Chapter 25 - We Are All Called to Be Teachers 171

Chapter 26 - The Footsteps of Your Heart on Land 179

Chapter 27 – The Song: Where Would I Have Been? 183

Chapter 28 - How Does One Walk With God? 185

PROLOGUE

A Simple Man's Walk with God - Extraordinary!

Jesus looked at them and said, "With man this is impossible, but with God all things are possible."

The collection of "God Stories" which the author, my friend and dear Sister in the Lord, Jannetta Collins-Johnson - shares from the pages of her simple everyday life experiences, serves as both a reminder and an encouragement to all who will walk for a while in her shoes by reading her book.

Ms. Collins-Johnson's "God Stories" - testimonies of what and how God accomplished mighty things in her life, reminds us that God really does use Ordinary people in Extraordinary ways. Like the apostles in the early church - who had no formal theological education or training, but walked with the Lord day and night and watched Him time and time again, do what to men was the impossible.
Sis. Jannetta Collins-Johnson, has no formal theological training, yet she raised five sons as a single mother. Extraordinary!

Barely able to keep food on the table for her own sons, she was frequently asked to feed and at times, house neighbours and strangers with no certainty of compensation. And though she didn't always know how she would manage, her simple walk with the Lord day in and day out, over the years taught her she could trust God - regardless of the assignment. And sure enough, time and time again, to her delight and personal spiritual growth and the amazement of others, Ms. Collins-Johnson shares with us stories of the Faithfulness of God and the timeliness of His Provisions time and time again. Extraordinary!

Writing a book is a daunting task - even for well-educated scholars, but the thought of an ordinary woman doing so is, simply - Extraordinary!

What readers must not miss in these stories of the extraordinary things God has done in the life of this ordinary woman, is the author's intent to share the stories in order to glorify God. In sharing these stories, Ms. Jannetta Collins-Johnson is really sharing with us how and why God does extraordinary things in the life of ordinary people.

How: God does extraordinary things in the life of ordinary people who submit to simply walking with and trusting Him day by day.
Why: Because God knows that those who experience Him doing extraordinary things - despite their simple, ordinary, humble lives, will give Him the glory He desires and deserves. The truth of the matter is God does the extraordinary in the lives of those who humble themselves before Him!

Finally, Jannetta Collins-Johnson's stories remind and encourage us that the Extraordinary becomes the Ordinary when we choose to Simply Walk with God.
"With man this is impossible, but with God all things are possible."

Rev. Dennis W. Mitchell
Atlanta, Georgia
November 2016

PREFACE

For many years I was blocked from working. Barriers were put up which I could not understand at the time, but now I know that this was part of a great testing, which was all part of God's Almighty plan. What God had been grooming me for was now to be disclosed as part of a bigger plan, which is centered on Jesus.

As I look back I am in awe at how it all happened. My biological children and I lived at home. From all appearances I was a single parent, but I have to give God praise and thanks for husbanding me and fathering my children, and as confirmation to this, He started using my home to house others.

It seems to me now, as I write, my 'Husband' opened the door for people to come in. It was the young, the old, the not so young, some sick, others well, but all needing care and/ or some type of assistance. Some came for a short time, others for longer periods. This home has many a story to tell. Through it all, God has done a mighty good job in taking me on a journey of faith. Many times someone would come asking for help, especially for help to mother their children and I would agree.

As they came so did the many promises of what they would contribute to the household in return, but we know too well that promises are promises and that they are not always kept. When the promises weren't kept, I could not say to the parents take your children and leave. In the midst of these situations, I experienced a great peace that enabled me to continue doing what I believed God had called me to do. The end result sometimes would be a thank you, other times not. Praise and thanks to God. He kept us. God has proven Himself to me to be my Provider, and much more. I saw God's awesomeness and His many attributes in this season.

I gave birth to six sons; my youngest son, named Teddy by his brother Ilya, was born prematurely and died at birth. My first born Nikita Dion Mark Johnson died at nineteen. This was very traumatic for the entire family. He was murdered without a cause and his death seemed senseless. My other sons are, in order of birth, Vivian Mark Johnson Jnr., Ilya Alaistair Mark Johnson, Lyle Peter Colin Johnson and Godfrey Jason St. Aubyn Mark. I thank God daily for my lovely sons and their families.

God placed in my home many sons and daughters to love, teach, encourage and discipline; a difficult, but beautiful experience, one that forced me to mature in Christ Jesus. It helped me to die to self, taught me sacrifice, and taught my children to share and to love, a feature that is sorely missing in today's society. I would always tell my sons beforehand when I had decided to take in a child. I never got a negative response from them on any occasion.

As a divorced parent with children to prepare for life, it was tough, trying to stretch the dollar while keeping focus on the values of the Word of God and not on the values the world forces upon you and your children. My sons now have many sisters and brothers who helped prepare them for their own families, by helping them learn how to care for younger ones as well. To this day they all love children and children are drawn to them.

A family unit with both parents can be challenging, more so a family unit with a single parent, so I relied a great deal upon God. I faltered many, many times trying to do it my way, which was the way of the world, so I fell, but I got up. Above God's way is the temptation to go the world's way; it actually makes you feel that this is the easier way. This is very far from the truth. The only way you have the confidence to hold on to the truth is keeping your focus on Almighty God, studying and doing His Word, staying in His presence and putting Him first in all things.

God's hand was upon me. I Praise and thank God for the truth that says "Train up a child in the way he should go, and when he is old he will not depart from it. Proverbs 22:6."

I had my losses but God's faithfulness is so powerful. He kept me and His Spirit never left me. The spirit of conviction was there making me feel that I could not continue with certain decisions that I made. There were times when I was restless, and I am evidence that God always gets His way. You can try to run, but you cannot hide.

God had to put me back on the narrow road in order to ensure that I fulfilled my purpose and destiny in Christ Jesus. I learned that my purpose and destiny is unique to me. No one else can fulfill my assignment for me. God created me for this purpose and I must walk this road. I had to take up my cross daily and follow Him and this prepared me for my Kingdom assignment.

I only truly found Peace when I recommitted my life to God and kept my gaze fully on my Lord and Saviour. I thought I was fine before, but when I experienced that peace, there was definitely a marked difference. I knew that I knew, without the shadow of a doubt that I was now on solid ground with my King of Kings and Lord of Lords. The Holy Spirit did His part and I had to do what I was called to do to remain in His presence.

I take this opportunity to thank God for placing me under His chosen vessel, Apostle Austin John de Bourg and the Ministry of Trinidad Christian Center. I knew the first time I spoke to the then Pastor de Bourg that this was the person of whom God spoke with the words "There is a man" who would help me. My Apostle, Pastor, Shepherd, Teacher, Prophet and Evangelist Austin John de Bourg is one who truly reflects God's image and likeness. I see him mostly as a spiritual grandpa. Mind you, he certainly is not the age of my grandparents but the wisdom etc. qualifies him.

For me grandparents are extremely precious persons, who are there to impart all the knowledge, experience and revelation to their dear grandchildren with much love. In my own life I never experienced grandparents, so I truly cherish this role.

I am truly thankful to God, our Apostle, our Pastor Kelvin Siewdass and all the ministers that faithfully make sure that the Word is delivered without alterations of any sort. We are fortunate to have the pure Word. We are encouraged, chastised when necessary, and praised during our walk. We are greatly loved by our leaders and this is the result of staying in God's Word and His presence.

I have many testimonies of God's greatness. These have spread far and wide. The hand of God extends to my biological children both here at home in Trinidad and Tobago and abroad to wherever they are. In most cases I cannot do it alone, as sometimes I need my sons' assistance. They are always willing and I thank them for their sharing and caring. They certainly are part of my ministry and I am thankful to God for them.

The desire of my heart is to always exalt the Name of Jesus which can only be done in obedience to His Word and in His presence and by reflecting Him in my life as I show forth His light on the earth during my walk with Him.

Contained in these pages to follow is a simple person's legacy to all who are willing to receive their place, joining me as an heir to God's great inheritance of love and purpose.

A SIMPLE MAN'S WALK WITH GOD

INTRODUCTION

[My Purpose, My Destiny.]

There has been much struggle within me, for years. I could identify with Moses when he was reluctant to step out in obedience when called by God. My feelings: "I cannot write! I do not have the ability! What should I write?" Or, "I am not sure what would cause this book to sell. Can I use names of people? What restrictions do I have?" Many things surfaced; doubt, fear, incapability. These were some of the things. Then, I was reminded about my first morning of God's grace concerning this book.

This took place very early one morning while visiting my son Godfrey in Washington D.C. I awoke praying in tongues. I prayed for a while and then I started getting a message that was so overwhelming that I recognized that I needed to get pen and paper to begin to document this assignment from God. These directions formed the written fabric of the book and outlined the direction the project was to take. God gave me the name of the book at that time as He dropped the words, "A Simple Man's Walk with God", into my spirit.

I showed my son the notes then and he was moved by it; but the more I thought about it fear stepped in and took hold of me. I could not bring myself to mention this to anyone else for years. I knew I would be laughed at. Somehow, I felt there must be an error. The wrong person was contacted. Fear gripped me and I felt incompetent. My thoughts "I have no qualifications, I am not a scholar, how can I do this? My life has been a life of hell. I have done some shameful things. I do not even have a job, and finance is not always available. I am not really a popular person - "in the limelight". It was an awkward feeling and for years I kept my silence, turning these things over and over in my mind.

Deep inside, I knew I had to get started, because it was not my doing, but God's doing. But the bigger question was "How could I get started?"

On a later trip to Washington D.C. during my quiet time with God, I got my deliverance from the spirit of fear, which was meant to destroy me and to significantly reduce the impact my testimony could have on countless who needed to make a decision for God. But I was reminded of what God wanted from me, and how it would be accomplished.

What I saw God emphasizing to me always was to stay in His Word and in His Presence. Staying in God's Word is so very important to our soul and spirit. Hebrews 4:12 & 13 reminds us of this:

"For the Word of God is quick and powerful and sharper than any two edged sword, piercing even to the dividing asunder of soul and spirit, and of the joints and marrow, and is a discerner of the thoughts and intents of the heart.

Neither is there any creature that is not manifest in His sight; but all things are naked and opened unto the eyes of Him with whom we have to do."

The Word of God can cut away at whatever will hold us back from fulfilling God's divine purpose and destiny for us. Therein lies our strength. "I can do all things through Christ who strengthens me" Philippians 4:13.

We are really so blessed to have not only the written Word – the Bible, but the ministry of the Word, where it is dissected and delivered to us. If we receive the ministry of the Word and allow it to go directly to our spirits, there will be a mighty impact on our lives. We would also experience emotional and other healing that is necessary before we can be successful in our Christian walk.

Many years ago God started teaching me obedience through His Holy Spirit. Through this teaching I started understanding the great role my mother played in laying the foundation for this very important role in my life. Discipline and obedience were a serious part of her training. She expected me to obey her and to learn from her example. My mother was disciplined in all that she did. This foundation that was laid would serve her future generations in a mighty way.

All who experienced her training appreciate the importance of obedience and discipline, and we see the need to pass this beautiful gift on to our children and grandchildren. Of course we falter, but because of the foundation that was laid, it is easier to return to operating in obedience and discipline.

My Mum was always hungry for more of God, and this important attribute she passed on to me by always having me accompany her on her visits to various churches. In her quest to draw closer and to be filled with God, she would visit other churches in addition to her home church. While she never left her congregation, she attended deliverance services where we experienced the mighty move of the Holy Spirit, and the manifested power of God. Years later, God took these seeds and used them to benefit His Kingdom.

This is when I saw that my earlier experiences were of great value. I could share from my experiences, because I felt what they felt. As God's children, He never allows our walk to go to waste for it is of prime importance to His Kingdom. In my own life I surely would not have been this far without Jesus, His Word and the Holy Spirit. My trials have been many and at times very harsh. As I look back now, I can see the hand of God was upon me and pulled me through in my seventy plus years of life, and is still taking me onward to fulfill my purpose and destiny.

Over ten years ago I had an experience that is hard for me to forget. I was slain in the spirit at my home during which time God spoke to me concerning my children and a few other areas. I did not know that God was about to make some changes in my life. During that season of my life I spent quite a lot of time in God's Word and in His presence. My church at that time was in an evangelistic thrust. I did not know then that God was preparing me for a dramatic move to my present assembly.

I got a few words from God that did not seem to be connected to anything in particular. I believe it may have been God the Father, and He said to me, "There will be a man". Few words they may have been, but spirit to spirit I understood a few things. I knew that God had a man to help me but in what way I did not know, but God allowed my spirit to trust Him.

My first test came early before I had fully transferred. This lying deceptive devil attempted to distract and take me off course, so he sent someone I knew well to try to deter me from taking the direction the Lord had begun to outline. This gentleman felt that he had my welfare at heart, but I knew that he was not the man the Lord sent to help me. As he began speaking, I told him I did not want to hear what he was saying (we were in his car on the highway and he was driving). He tried to proceed and the words that came from me were, "If you go on I will jump out of this car". I did not want to hear any negative words, because it was not coming from God.

Normally I am a very calm person so I believe he was so shocked that he was very quiet for a long while. I eventually broke the silence explaining that I will only trust God on this move. I knew God had initiated the move and it was not up for debating.

Over time the former church brother, mentioned earlier, continued both privately and publicly, to challenge my decision to move from my current church, but divine intervention always took place and the plan to derail me was destroyed. The move could have destroyed my walk with God, but God had a man, a mighty man of God; a man filled with God's Word who willingly carried his cross while staying in God's presence. Father God locked a vision within me for this servant of His and his ministry and I knew that this man, then Pastor Austin John de Bourg, was the person whom the Lord sent to help me and not the false prophet who tried to destroy my walk.

As I look back I am sure that Father God locked that vision for this His son and the ministry into me and sealed it.

Another major part of my purpose is to nurture and encourage those who need help to mature in Christ, and to those who are not in Christ as well who need encouragement. They might have the desire in their heart, but because of the earthly burdens and baggage they might be carrying, they need encouragement and some guidance to keep growing in Christ. It only became obvious to me recently when I recognized that there was a pattern and people would be placed

around me. God would either point them out to me or connect them through a situation where they needed assistance. The role is likened to that of a mother: to love, nurture, encourage, discipline and whatever else I am guided to do, more on a one to one basis.
I am privileged to have sons and daughters that I did not physically birth, but they are sons and daughters never the less. God Himself made these connections and they have proven themselves to be my spiritual children.

I have lost count of the number of children God placed in my home, but I ask God's blessings upon them all, from time to time. As I took a count of these children who lived with me, I believe I got to thirty and still counting.

There were times of joy and times of sadness, but all in all lots of times to be remembered. I can call to mind an occasion when God orchestrated to have one of the loveliest children come to my home.

A wall in my home became very porous and needed to be replaced. We got a few estimates, this particular estimate seemed to top the list, it was neither the lowest nor the highest, but once again God had a plan. This team was recommended and we went along with them.

I was told when they started that they did not have a job, and they prayed and fasted to get a job, and this was the answer to their prayer.

As the job progressed, one day, one of the brothers started telling me about a situation with a child. I listened and I thought, "What does this have to do with me?" I listened quietly. I did not say much, but my mind started racing as I heard the report.

I can get very upset when children are involved. It affects me deep within my spirit and I feel that I can rescue them all. I would normally get the urging for the ones that I can help. The others I just have to leave alone.

It appeared to me that this guy summed up all that he saw and realized that here was an opportunity to rescue his daughter, so he took full advantage of the situation. Finally he made his plea with a direct question, "Would you keep my daughter for me?" I was still silent. I never rush to answer questions; that is my normal response. Maybe I like to have them register before I answer. By this time I started hearing all the promises, which I learned not to pay any attention to, since this would not have been the reason for assisting. I finally answered him, telling him I would pray about it, even though I felt deep inside I would be having the child come to my home.

He brought the child a few days later. She was muscular in build, had a rugged look with a low unkempt hair cut, yet there was a special beauty about her. Her build and the hair cut made her look like an athlete which might make you afraid to upset her in anyway. She looked quite capable of beating you up, but the opposite was the case. She was kind hearted, gentle, and a loving spirit, always ready to help and to make sacrifices for anyone. She had not been to school much, but showed signs of being intelligent, with a great deal of common sense and street sense which she often utilized. She made use of every opportunity presented to her, and she saw the sky as her limit. She loved the Lord and this helped her greatly.

Unfortunately after several years, I allowed her to be disrupted, and while she received a lot to take her through, she was not able to continue on her course after she left my home. She has fought good and hard to stand. I give her full credit for her accomplishment. I can see God getting great testimony from her life. She always reflects on what she learned in those four to five years, and says that she would not forget it.

She had struggles, but she had proven many things to me. While she was not the only one that I saw blossom with love and care, her progress was extremely quick. She readily received and had a drive within her to succeed. I saw what LOVE can accomplish. I saw love heal, break down barriers, throw down walls, and give you wings to fly.

I thank God for every opportunity He has given me to be of assistance to someone. My greatest satisfaction is being able to honour my Lord by helping someone to experience His love. To me this is a great honour, just to be considered for this purpose. I have highlighted this child, but each one has an interesting story to tell. I enjoyed them all and they are all dear to my heart. Some were more challenging than others; she was one of my groomers, put here to test my patience.

I liken my response to these beautiful ones to that of salvation. As I look back, it all began with my upbringing and my dear parents. Their response I believe was propelled either by teaching from their home and/or the love of God. My mother always seemed to be willing to help when there was a need. I learned from what I heard or saw, then accepting that God would want me to assist. Once this was settled I accepted the responsibility for the child or adult (as it was sometimes), then allowed God to guide me with respect to what needed to be done for that particular individual to help them be what God wanted them to be. Sometimes it was very difficult, and at times I was not even sure what God wanted, but believing that He was in control, helped.

Willingness to wait on God's instructions for each person in my care had to be consistent and the love for God had to be my driving force. Service to others requires sacrifice and we must be willing mentors for the children and adults God places in our lives.

[Prayer]

Loving Father, as this book is read I ask you to capture the hearts and the spirits of the readers setting them free from any strongholds or barriers or any hindrances that's blocking them from going forward or from knowing you as Lord and Saviour. Release the spirit of praise, worship and thanksgiving as you renew minds and soften hearts. Draw each reader to Yourself as they learn to love you with all their heart, soul, mind and strength. Thank you for all that You have given to us and help us to use it for your glory. In Jesus' Name, Amen

CHAPTER ONE

[Supernatural Walk]

As we go through challenges in life, a supernatural walk can be an exciting and stimulating experience with many rewards. This can only be appreciated by a simple man who has the spirit of a child, trusting and free with the Father and Lord Jesus the Christ, at the helm.

As a child builds relationships, either with parents or care givers, a bond is formed. The basis of that bond is Agape (God's love), and the child places all trust in those who are close to the child.

Trust, the greatest asset of a child's development, is exhibited when that child, [especially those with whom that bond is formed], would jump fearlessly from any height fully expecting to be caught.
Children trust and act in a loving way until they begin to be influenced by society. At that time changes may occur.

A simple man, like a child, can be a subtle and unassuming 'weapon' in the hands of God. On the surface easily taken for granted, or underestimated, regarding their level of knowledge and understanding. We simple men serve a unique and loving Saviour with conditions and guidelines to guide our pathway.

Mark 10:15 tells us "Assuredly, I say to you, whoever does not receive the Kingdom of God as a little child, will by no means enter it." NKJV. What does this mean? We need to become as a child putting away all our hang-ups, frills and societal habits, bending our knees in submission to the King of Kings and Lord of Lords, and trusting Him all the way.

God knows just what is needed for our acceptance into the Kingdom, and for us to live a supernatural life. This is the reason that He gives us the simple requirement of trusting. As we trust, we are expected to accept His gift of His only begotten Son Jesus, who died that we might have life more abundantly. He took all our sin upon Himself freeing us to take this supernatural walk. Any other decision will hold us back from this beautiful relationship with Christ Jesus.

We have access to the supernatural ABBA FATHER, SAVIOUR, THE I AM, BIG BROTHER, GREAT TEACHER, GUIDE, COUNSELOR, DELIVERER, HEALER, PEACE MAKER, PROVIDER, RESTORER, JOY GIVER and many other attributes in the triune Godhead-Father, Son and Holy Spirit. The Holy Spirit enhances and enables our lives tremendously meeting all our needs. It was compulsory for Jesus to go, so that He could send the Holy Spirit to come and reside in us. Even though Jesus our Lord, Creator of the heavens and the earth, showed us how to live a supernatural life by trusting the Father with and in all things, it would have been totally impossible without Him in our lives. As we acknowledge Lord Jesus as Saviour of our lives, and take His example of putting the Kingdom of God first at all times, we will certainly show the world His example of obedience, trust, and love for the Father and for each other.

God promises us this very life and empowers us through His Holy Spirit to accomplish it. We are reminded that His was flawless, and in Him ours can be also.

David was a great example of simplicity, possessing all the characteristics for Israel's king. However, since his father and brothers saw him as inferior, he was not even considered.

Utilizing David's experiences as a shepherd boy in the field, God fashioned and groomed him for his future assignment as King. In so doing, God taught us that His vision for us is different from ours. Being a heart God, He disregards the outer appearance of man to work at and display a special quality. We look at the outward appearance, but He looks far deeper at the heart. Praise God. God knew that as David trusted Him in the role of a shepherd boy, he would also trust Him when he became King.

The supernatural, simple man's walk is perfected in Jesus Christ.

There is nothing sweeter or more fulfilling than walking with God, even with the challenges one will encounter along the way, with the understanding and assurance that we have a promise of hope and victory in Jesus as we reign in and with Him in victory.

It may not always appear that way, especially if we are not on this committed path. In my own journey, over many years I did not quite understand how fulfilling and desirable walking with God could be. I was so incapable of trusting Him fully to lead me always, so I encountered great confusion, making a mess of things. Praise God! I now understand surrender. I still make mistakes, but as I get better at allowing Him to lead, I am filled with His Peace that passes all understanding.

Oh! The love of Christ that I experience because Christ Jesus shed His blood for me, so, we too as His children can spread His love throughout the world. It is only with this love that you can see the unlovely as lovable.. The way I see things now can only be seen through His eyes, understanding when God said, in Proverbs 3 vs. 5" Trust in the Lord with all your heart, and lean not on your own understanding; in all your ways acknowledge Him, and He shall direct your paths." NKJV.

Praise God! It is never too late to start this beautiful journey. I am so excited about my walk with Jesus as my Lord and Master, I can now appreciate such beauty in His creation.

I encourage the young ones, not to waste their youth wandering in the wilderness of life, dissatisfied, grumbling, rebellious and ungrateful. If they do live like this, life is made much tougher than it was meant to be, and one ends up facing an uncertain future. The scriptures are true. Once we determine to start this walk, we can choose eternal life with Jesus or eternal death without Him.

We can be spared so many head and heart aches if we just stay in the Word of God. When we abide in the Word, we are put in the position of the overcomer in whom fears and other crippling spirits cannot reside.

We have evaded the Word of God far too long, attending church services faithfully, but that is as far as we are prepared to go. This has greatly contributed to the failure of the Church, and all over the world we are now seeing the consequences of this lack. In some instances, generations are lost to crime and other illegal activities and their only hope for deliverance is returning to the Lord Jesus Christ in spirit and in truth.

We are now called to revisit our foundation. The truth and power that the early church experienced through their walk with Almighty God has been lost to us. What caused their power to be witnessed in such depth? What caused them to stand the test of time? The disciples were not afraid to give up their lives joyfully, all for the cause of Christ! It is of vital importance for us to get back into His Word and in His presence, in order to build a deep relationship with Jesus our Lord and Saviour, which will result in trusting Him deeply.

Obedience comes easily as a result of that trust.

The psalmist wrote in Ps. 119: 105 "Your Word is a lamp unto my feet and a light for my path." Oh if we could grasp what the Word can and will do for us if we will only take it, believe and apply it to our daily living.

These words, from 1995 Integrity's Hosanna! Music CD came from a popular song and they are powerful and true words:

> *"In Your presence that's where I am strong; In Your presence, O Lord my God.*
> *In Your presence that's where I belong; seeking Your face, touching Your Grace in the cleft of the Rock, in Your presence Oh God."*

As we stay in God's Word and in His presence, we will trust Him because we will know Him, and would build a deep relationship with Him. There would always be challenges, and some of these will come in the form of doubt and fear, but with the knowledge of the Word, and with the Father, Jesus the Son and the Holy Spirit living inside of us, we would surely be able to stand.

We would stand believing God's Word and would be able to declare that we are more than conquerors. Without the Word we cannot declare our victory. This can only happen if we stay in God's Word and in His presence. This is when we experience great joy and contentment, knowing that Jesus would never leave us nor forsake us.

If you have started on this walk, but you are not fully committed like I was I invite you to take the opportunity now to surrender all to Him; let it be from the heart so that you will once again take on His image and likeness and receive the benefits of being a son/daughter.

Total surrender produces a willing and submissive heart of Divine Love. What a wonderful gift given to us by our Lord and Saviour Jesus Christ who awaits us with outstretched arms filled with His Agape Love.

This supernatural walk is based upon and only fulfilled as a result of "HIS LOVE".

For those who have not accepted Jesus Christ as Lord, you must first believe that Jesus Christ came to the earth as the Son of God, shed His blood and died for you and arose from the grave so that you can have eternal life. Receiving Jesus Christ as your Lord and Saviour is a simple but profound heart decision. This is the most important decision that I have ever made in my life; this is definitely priceless.

"Tis so sweet to trust in Jesus, just to take Him at His Word."

Submission is one of our mighty weapons of destruction to the old life style. Heaven rejoices as the whistle is blown to start this sweet love relationship with our Lord Jesus Christ. As we experience this relationship, we receive revelation of the triune God; Almighty Father, Son Jesus, and His Holy Spirit as His infinite Grace and Mercy protects us. Now we can say, "But for His Grace and Mercy"! I know I certainly could have been destroyed, were it not for God's mighty hand upon me ensuring fulfillment and revealing His plan and purpose before my eyes.

Sometimes we have to wrestle with Him like Jacob did saying, God I will not let go, I need you to take me through, so I can be on my way. Once we start on this journey, nothing or no one, not even our weaknesses must ever have the power of preventing us from completing the walk.

This journey is about obeying without knowing what the outcome of that obedience can be. Walking by faith, trusting and allowing the Spirit of God to lead us, even without the understanding , complements our divine faith walk. Giving up of self, as much as it may hurt, gets easier when we realize that we own nothing or no one, but we are owned by Someone who paid an exceptional price for us. Even time is not ours. To make it simple, we become His and all that we think and have belongs to Him.

As we become vessels of honour, we may have to undertake strange activity that people may not understand. However, if we say that we love the Lord with all our heart, soul, mind and strength then we have to prove our love to Him through our obedience.

It is supernatural because of a supernatural God, and 2 Chronicles 7:14 proves this as it says, "If my people who are called by my name, will humble themselves, and pray and seek my face, and turn from their wicked ways, then I will hear from heaven, and will forgive their sin and heal their land."

God is searching for true worshippers, those who will worship Him in Spirit and in truth. All of creation is waiting for the sons of God to arise and take their rightful positions. This will impact the world in a mighty way. Lives will be changed and conditions and attitudes will improve as we experience the presence of God.

There is a beautiful image at the Centre of Excellence in Macoya, which is visible from the highway going to and from Piarco Airport. It is a beautifully designed/ well groomed flag of Trinidad and Tobago. On each journey to and from the east, it remains an exciting moment for me to look upon the beauty, grace and elegance of this imposing landmark. This flag just flows with the wind. What I see in the flag is the way God wants us to be, willing to flow with Him as He pleases, allowing Him to move freely in our lives as He flows in us and we flow in Him.

What a spectacle it would be for the world to see the sons of God arising. I yearn to be like that flag in the hands of my Master and Lord, and I pray that we could all get to that place soon because the world needs it urgently.

God is preparing a people in this time for this supernatural walk. You and I are included among those people so do not let it be too late to get on the ark. Decide to be an instrument to go and to do whatever He wants and to be used for His Glory. The beauty is that we can achieve this, if we die to self. We must truly die in order to live for Him, but we must see it as priority. I pray that you will be encouraged as I too am encouraged to fulfill this supernatural walk with God at the helm.

Almighty Father in the name of Jesus the Christ, I join forces with You, and I ask You to remove and destroy every hindrance that is blocking us from walking this supernatural walk. Help us Holy Spirit where we are weak, keep us focused and be with us as we make decisions that will be of benefit for the Kingdom's sake. Amen.

CHAPTER TWO

[Grace!!! Guards and Guides]

Scripture records that obedience brings blessings. We have promises that are released upon us when we adhere to the commandments of God. These are considered blessings.

How, then, can we explain those times when we are in total disobedience to God, even when we try to frustrate his plans, we can still clearly see His hand pushing and pulling things in place for us? At these times it is GRACE, God's unmerited favour, extended to us either directly from God and/or indirectly through man.

The law came through Moses but grace and truth came through Jesus Christ.

God's Grace is sufficient for us. Paul tells us from his experience in 2 Corinthians 12: 9 "My Grace is sufficient for you, for my strength is made perfect in weakness." This says that when we are in need of strength God is our source and His provision of strength is unlimited. God often provides and extends a mighty hand towards us even when we are not aware that we are in need.

Before coming to Christ, God in His Love keeps us under His hand of safety, to protect His purpose in us. In His goodness, the Spirit draws us and we are led to repentance, fulfilling salvation. As we respond and accept the sacrificial gift of Jesus Christ, our Lord and Saviour, who gave His life for us, we are sure to gain entry into the

Kingdom of God.

> *Romans 2:4 "Or do you despise the riches of His goodness, forbearance and long suffering, not knowing that the good ness of God leads you to repentance?"*

Do you see God's goodness, mercy and grace flowing all over your life? As you look back, even before accepting Jesus Christ as Lord and Saviour, what do you see? As I look back at many areas of my life, I just stop and lift up my heart and hand in praise and thanksgiving to Him for keeping me during the periods of my stupidity. Like many people who ended up in a hard place (for some it was the mental hospital), I was on my way there at one point of my life, but by the hand of God, I was delivered and set free.

I remember in my time of marital problems especially after my divorce, men were trying to befriend me. They had all the "sweet talk" that is usually extended and even desired at this vulnerable time. However, I know that grace was at work, and mercy said "NO". Many proposals for sexual dalliances were put forward, such as, "no one will know, we could go out of town where people would not know us". I refused! Years later, I am still thanking Him for saving my life and His purpose for me. I could have contracted AIDS and died. I am sure that God's guidance and protection was surrounding me. That definitely is the hand of Grace.

We are not all called to be intellectuals, but we are all called to walk with God, under His guidance, and His grace takes care of it all.

> *Proverbs 4:18. "But the path of the just is like the shining sun, that shines ever brighter unto the perfect day."*

God will keep His loved ones bright and shining. This is the power of grace even when we stray off God's course temporarily. I am not saying that it is okay to deliberately come off course and God will keep you safe. I know of persons, who never got back on course, so please do not test God. We never know what the future holds for us, so stay on His salvation path.

In running the good race we are dependent on God's Grace. We cannot even start, much less complete it, without His keeping power. His blood is also necessary to cleanse us as we go, and His Holy

Spirit to guide us through to the end. Jesus made the way where there seemed to be no way for us and He brought us into this time of Grace as He fulfilled the law. His righteousness is part of the Grace package, so we become the Righteousness of God only in Christ Jesus. This is our aid for living right.

We must rely on His righteousness for this good race, because we can only live right for God as we obtain the righteousness of God through and in His Son Christ Jesus.

Sometimes in the midst of my trials, I could feel the arms of love around me, reminding me that He has me in the palm of His hand, and that He will never leave me nor forsake me. In testing times, you may not want to go to someone for help, but God in His mercy will send help through a stranger, just at the right time. So that you will know without a doubt that God's hand is upon you.

Grace allows us to take on God's character, and calls or guides us to obedience.

I was at a point of my life where I was walking with God, but I was procrastinating about something that seemed to me could wait; this therefore was my decision. I suffered with a back problem for many years, which caused me much pain and many months on traction both at home and in the hospital as the condition worsened. I was referred to a Neurosurgeon to get an opinion, possibly for surgery or some other form of management. He advised surgery and this required a follow up visit, but deep inside I felt this was not the way I should go so I never went back to the doctor. I cannot say God told me, but I felt God would heal me, and truly one day I realized I was totally healed, and never had another episode of that problem. As I obeyed and did what I was called to do, God's healing hands touched me. This did not happen in a prayer line, through the laying on of hands or calling for the elders.

In demonstration of His love, God encourages us through His divine favour to grow in obedience. As God covers us in His grace, we are assisted to give up habitual sin and we rise to victory over death, hell and the grave.

With Father, Son and the Holy Spirit dwelling in us, His character is more evident and we experience power over our enemies as they become our foot stool, under our feet, or even behind us.

In God's wisdom, He allows us to experience many life issues, some more challenging than others, but all necessary for growth. Grace protects us from ourselves, since most times we are our greatest enemies. The lessons may be hard at times, but in the end when we reflect, we see God's love and favour shining through giving us a glorious victory.

In a short period of time, I experienced deaths of many close loved ones. They came fast and furious; some I was prepared for because of illness, but most of them were unexpected.

My sister, sister in law, brother, aunt, very close friends, then my youngest son's dad. This was devastating to me, but God in His love worked things out in a way that buffeted some of the pain. I saw my youngest son's Dad as my best friend and the love of my life and in a way idolized him, so God intervened, by cutting off our intimate relationship preparing me for a permanent separation. This was one death that I did not expect, and as was said by one of his friends, "He was so full of life; I did not think that he would die." I was so thankful to God for His move, because the pain I felt would have been many times worse if God did not take things in His hands some time before. I thought I made a decision, but I know grace abounded as we remained close friends. This was a challenging time in itself, (I got to a place where I felt I did not deserve to live), but for God and His love.

I give God praise and thanks for His love and order. As I look back, (on reflection,) this seemed to be a trial run for the following year when again suddenly I lost my first born son through tragic circumstances. This was even more difficult. I felt one day I would awake from this dream. I went through the motions, and you know what - I overcame. Thank God! I learned, among other things, that nothing or no one should be more important to me than my Lord and Saviour Jesus Christ, a gracious and merciful God, who holds the future.

This was an extremely rough time for me, but I am sure that I would never have been where I am now if circumstances remained as they were. It was a necessary evil that God turned around for His good by protecting His call on my life as He made

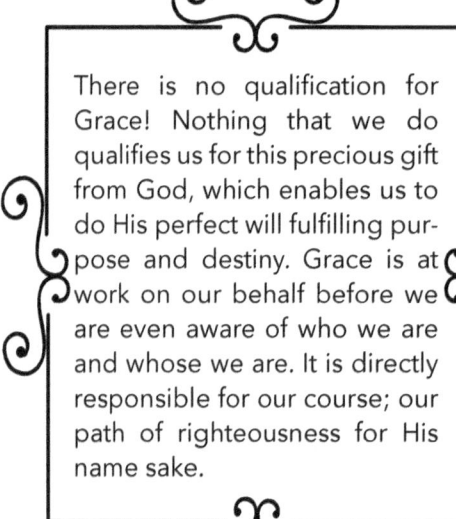

these changes, and it surely was not up to me. I just had to trust Him and go along with His plan. His Grace was sufficient for me in my time of distress, and He turned all things over for good because of my love for Him, which was also grace.

There is no qualification for Grace! Nothing that we do qualifies us for this precious gift from God, which enables us to do His perfect will fulfilling purpose and destiny. Grace is at work on our behalf before we are even aware of who we are and whose we are. It is directly responsible for our course; our path of righteousness for His name sake.

Let us not take God's Grace for granted and be thankful and comply by returning His precious love. He has the blue print for the finished project and knows what is best for us. Be reminded that God will always have His way. It is my experience that if we do not submit and come willingly, we will come painfully, but successfully for God's Kingdom.

My prayer is that we will allow God to have HIS way in our lives without resisting Him.

Gracious, precious Father help us to understand Your love for us, and that grace is surely Your hand guarding and guiding us in this life. Open our spiritual eyes, ears and heart with divine understanding and wisdom to see our need of the importance of allowing Your grace to guard and guide us into the Master's arms, purpose and will. Thank You loving Father for grace that enables us to trust You in all Your ways in Jesus Christ precious, holy and worthy name. Amen.

CHAPTER THREE

[Faith]

Faith, I believe, is really a matter of life and death in the life of a Believer. As we go through certain experiences, we have an opportunity to exhibit faith in God and in prayer. Faith in God can lead us unto death like Abel or to life like Noah (Genesis 7:1-16) and Enoch (Gen 5:24); bear in mind that even though Abel was led to death through his faith in God, he is no less a faith hero than Noah or Enoch.

How are we doing in our faith walk? Are we experiencing ridicule by our family and those around us because of the decisions that we make? Oh yes! Sometimes by our own brothers and sisters in the Kingdom who do not feel the same way as we do because their faith may be different.

In your time of weakness, do you sometimes feel the need for someone to join their faith with yours, but find it difficult to find someone? In these times, remember you and God are a majority. Jesus, our divine intercessor, along with the cloud of witnesses in heaven is still actively cheering us on. Among them is Father Abraham, and beautiful Sarah who is still smiling. But you know what? Because of her mighty experience of faith, instead of smiling because she doubted God, she now has a victorious smile.

I too would love to exhibit such a victorious smile that pleases my Abba.

My heart's desire for my ex-husband was for him to experience the true life that I experienced because of the love of the Lord Jesus Christ, the Father and the Holy Spirit. This is a life of perfect freedom in Christ. This is life eternal, which is different from that of the world. The world's accomplishments are not lasting, whereas accomplishments in God are everlasting.

My husband and I were married for about eight years. We lived together for five of those eight years. In this union we gave birth to four sons, three sons were born within twenty three months (1st birthday -3rd birthday) and the fourth was born in the fourth year.

> I was happy that in spite of the physical abuse, my child and I survived. I thank God because the pain, bitterness, unforgiveness and all that usually accompanies this type of treatment, did not remain with me.

Our marriage was one of turmoil. This was due to the fact that my husband was an alcoholic. This disease not only affected our marriage, but did great damage to his personality, and it began affecting my personality as well.

I took my marriage vows seriously, (I would dare say that he took them seriously to a point as well), and felt that if I endured the abuse and life style, things would change. After years my personality started changing. At first I did not recognize this, but when I did, I had to struggle to keep my sanity. In the midst, I truly felt that each day would be different, and that somehow things would turn around. It was an act of faith. I saw my husband waking up one day and coming to his right senses.

One day I came face to face with death, and had to make a decision as to whether I wanted to live or die. Of course I chose life! I needed to live, and my children needed me alive. At this time I was on my fourth pregnancy. I was happy that in spite of the physical abuse, my child and I survived. I thank God because the pain, bitterness, unforgiveness and all that usually accompanies this type of treatment, did not remain with me. We were separated for a while, until he finally migrated. After a few years I saw no change, so my father in law assisted me in obtaining a divorce.

My heart was grieved though, for my husband had much ability and great potential, yet the talent I recognized in him seemed to be going to waste. I thought at least if he migrated, there would be some motivation to do better and for a while it appeared so, but on his return, things seemed worse.

My desire and prayer for him never changed; that he would come to know Jesus Christ as Lord and that he would find God's purpose and destiny for his life. Unfortunately, after many years, I saw much deterioration in all areas of his life. We kept in touch and I would visit at times with my sons and their families. Somehow I still had hope.

> So comfortable was I in that knowledge that I gave him room to receive the ministry in the way which was most comfortable for him.

A number of years ago, under the guidance of the Holy Spirit, I willingly journeyed to San Fernando for almost a week. My Lord directed me to go and witness to him about the love of God and Jesus' sacrifice for us. It was a pleasure to share with him and his partner. They were both happy that I was there as usual, and I was free to share with them what I felt led to share. While he heard, and there were no obvious signs of resistance, his partner was open to the Spirit of God, and was willing to receive the counsel that was offered. She definitely wanted what was offered, but was hesitant because of his response. He took it very lightly and in fact made several jokes about the matter during our conversations. He showed some curiosity concerning alcohol and a few other areas, asking if there was any record in the scriptures. Alcoholism was his major outward show of his inner problem. At the end of those days I left him in the hands of our Lord and Saviour Jesus Christ, knowing many seeds had been planted.

Shortly after this occasion, a team of Believers was about to visit our church assembly. It consisted of persons who were delivered from drugs, alcohol and all the habits that went with these lifestyles. Some of these men spent years in mental institutions, prisons and other facilities as a result of their habits. I was led to invite my ex-husband and his partner to the worship service. To my surprise, he accepted and traveled thirty plus miles to the service. There were some obstacles to his getting there. On arrival he said, "I am here as a spectator and nobody is to put their hand on me". I smiled on the inside, knowing that God was in control and the devil a true liar from the pit of hell. I knew that my GOD had a plan if not he would not be there. I knew it was God who brought him, and the Spirit is the one who draws us. So comfortable was I in that knowledge that I gave him room to receive the ministry in the way which was most comfortable for him.

Again I saw that his partner wanted to move forward, but he was a hindrance. She was humiliated by him and so she did not respond. She received the seeds planted and finally left the rocky relationship of many years soon after. She is now happily married and serving God.

But, Praise God! Seeds were planted in him as well and I continued to visit with him occasionally. He thought he was in control and professed that all was well with him. He continued to live his life as he chose and God continued to stay in control as He always does.

A number of years had now passed and life went on as usual. One of our sons got a call that his dad was in hospital. On his arrival in San Fernando he found his father at home. He had been discharged from the hospital.

He joked about the reason for his visit to the hospital. Speaking to me on the phone, he said, "I got up and just could not remember who was supposed to be in the house with me so I chased everybody out." If he had had too much alcohol this would be his typical behaviour, but this seemed different, he was alcohol free. The doctors said everything was fine and they sent him home.

His condition worsened, however, and he was getting weak. Our sons would visit him. I was on my way to the U.S.A. and the morning I was leaving I spoke to him as they were taking him back to the hospital. I kept talking to him and I would always pray with him. At this time we all felt this was the effect of years of excess alcohol, but my son was very concerned, when he recognized that he was losing his grip, and was not able to feed himself and was also unable to control his saliva. There was cause for concern.

He was admitted to hospital and after further testing, the diagnosis was a tumor on the brain. He got progressively worse, but there was hope that with surgery all would be well. My son who lives in the United States and is a doctor, spoke with his doctor who assured him that he had a great chance because of where the tumor was located. He said once the pressure was released all would be well. They were awaiting a bed in the Intensive care unit so the surgery was booked for four days away. The day before the surgery, my son in Trinidad called me and was crying. He had just received a call from the hospital saying that Dad had died. He didn't know what to do.

At this time, my concern was not so much that he had died, but about his soul. I knew God was in control, and while I was not anxious, I was concerned.

A day after his death, another son called me and told me that a lady had come to his father's house and told him that God had sent her to visit him. She visited him about three or four times before he died. (Incidentally these visits started several months before he died and several years after he had visited my church.)

She was someone who knew my husband and his family as a child and had played in a carnival band that the family produced. I would like you to visualize this. You have not seen someone for many years nor have you been thinking of that person, then suddenly you awake one morning calling that person's name. Why? Why? You don't even know where this person is?!

So she inquired from the Lord and realized that she was to visit with him. She spoke to her husband letting him know what was happening and they decided to make enquires to find out where he was. After receiving the information, she did what she felt the Lord Almighty directed her to do.

Be mindful that God has co-heirs all over and His friends are many.

No one knew at that time that God was preparing to take him home. Five or six months after her first visit, she went to visit again to find that this was a different person she was seeing. He was not well at this time and needed to be taken back to the hospital. God had been ministering to him and he was now willing to accept Jesus Christ as Lord.

Two days prior to his departure, God gave her directions to go and anoint him for his journey. God's love, mercy and grace are so real. His arms are outstretched to us and we should not wait until it is too late to accept the opportunity to exhibit his true image and likeness to others. If only we would just open our hearts and receive what He has so freely given to us sooner rather than later. In His mercy and His grace, He accepts the deathbed confession of faith in salvation; but we forfeit opportunities to walk in our purpose and destiny exhibiting to the world His love, while storing up our treasures in heaven. Each one of God's children has an assignment to fulfill. Wherever we are, God has someone for us to affect. It is our choice if we respond or not. If we do, we through the Holy Spirit will bring glory and honour to His Name.

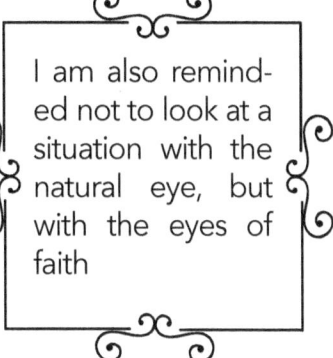

I am also reminded not to look at a situation with the natural eye, but with the eyes of faith

According to Hebrews 11:1 "Faith is the substance of things hoped for; the evidence of things not seen". This experience with my ex-husband, Mark, expanded my belief in keeping focused on God's Word and His promises to His children. Even with the divorce I see God honouring our union. This experience is a beautiful example of God giving me the desire of my heart after having prayed without ceasing. I am also reminded not to look at a situation with the natural eye, but with the eyes of faith. It also strengthens my promise like Joshua, that "As for me and my household, we will serve the Lord". As a result of this, I can use this testimony to assist those that God would bring in my path.

"Looking unto Jesus, the Author and Finisher of our Faith, who for the joy that was set before Him, endured the cross, despising the shame and has sat down at the right hand of the throne of God"- Hebrews 12:2.

Because of my first hand experience, I can say with certainty that I truly believe the scripture in Acts 16:31, "So they said, "Believe on the Lord Jesus Christ, and you will be saved, you and your household.""

This was the answer that Paul and Silas gave to the keeper of the prison, when he thought that they had all escaped. He awoke and found the doors open and assuming the prisoners had escaped, he drew his sword to kill himself, but he was stopped by them when they spoke out. "Do yourself no harm, for we are all here." The keeper's question to them, "Sirs, what must I do to be saved?" He believed their answer and truly he and his household were not only saved but baptized as well. What a mission of faith! You too can experience this faith.

Heavenly Father I thank you for these experiences. While they were difficult at times, You took them and used them for Your glory and to help others to see Your goodness and love. You certainly show us how much Grace abounds, and that You are in total control always. You have called us to seek Your face, to love You and our fellow man. Loving Father we need Your help. As we read this chapter, use it to release the Spirit of faith to all around. Help us to stay in Your Word and trust You in all circumstances. We thank You that You hear and surely answer us in Jesus Christ precious name we pray. Amen.

CHAPTER FOUR

[Fear vs. Faith]

Our walk with God is by faith and not by sight. We hear this all the time but do we really pay attention to what is being said? Whatever is obvious or can be seen is always easy to believe. With faith, as we believe, we see. If I were to say to you that Jesus is returning soon, you would probably laugh at me if you have not been studying the scriptures and believing the Word of God, which develops our faith. We develop faith by hearing the Word of God. As we believe what we hear it becomes easy for us to be in agreement with God and to understand and not take His Word for granted.

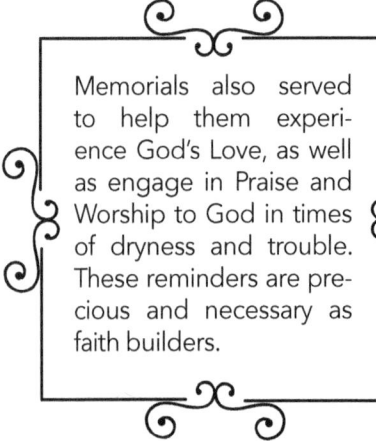

Memorials also served to help them experience God's Love, as well as engage in Praise and Worship to God in times of dryness and trouble. These reminders are precious and necessary as faith builders.

There are times in our walk when we are sure the presence of God is with us, yet there are other times when we do not feel His presence at all. King David, the devoted worshipper, experienced aloneness and so did Jesus in the garden, while on His way to the cross. Psalm 22: 1, "My God, My God, why have you forsaken me? Why are you so far from helping me?" In this Psalm, King David cries out to God, so did Jesus, but did they not believe? What do we do in such a time? Do we give up and withdraw? No we should not. We have to stand on His Word and press on while believing His Word, "I will never leave you nor forsake you." It is at these moments of perceived abandonment that we need to reflect on God's goodness, to remind ourselves of His Love, His Grace and His Mercy. In this regard scripture tells us that God told the children of Israel to build memorials; as they continued on their journey, so that they would remember to teach their children about His love, and the mighty things He had done for them. Memorials also served to help them experience God's Love, as well as engage in Praise and Worship to God in times of dryness and trouble. These reminders are precious and necessary as faith builders.

Romans 10: 17 says "So then faith comes by hearing, and hearing by the Word of God." Our hearts must be open and receptive to God's word. Otherwise, we can be like many who hear but do not experience the fullness of God; as happened even in Jesus' time. (e.g. the Pharisees and Sadducees, the religious leaders of Jesus' time.)

There is natural faith that we all must have to be able to exist comfortably in the world. It takes faith to believe that the plane in which we fly will not crash. We require faith for all that we do. A child is born and without being taught operates in faith. He or she has faith in those people who are around them especially parents or caregivers. Because of this trust, sometimes they are abused. When playing with my own children, they would jump without any warning expecting to be caught, and you had better catch them. What trust they exhibit, not realizing the danger!

We have a surety in Christ Jesus who went to the Cross and died, enduring all the suffering, pain, shame and disgrace for us. Through His resurrected life we must believe and accept what He did for us so that we may have eternal life. This, to most people, is too simple to be understood. Some believed Jesus was even less than an ordinary child, because he was born in a stable, wrapped in swaddling clothes and lying in a manger, with no fuss or pomp. After all, the Jews expected a King in all of his glory to be their Messiah who would come and rescue them. He could never be the one, represented in such a simple form.

This God kind of faith that we are speaking of is supernatural. The more we study the Word, the more assurance we have that our faith will increase. Faith helps us to move mountains and challenge the devil whenever he tries to hinder our walk with God. Faith comes from God. It is a blessing to the believer.

The devil comes to extinguish our faith and replace it with fear. Fear comes in all forms, prettily disguised by the enemy and the satanic world, preventing us from reaching or striving to reach our potential in Jesus. Fear destroys purpose and destiny. It attacks the mind and is intended to cripple us, rendering us helpless and hopeless, causing us to take our eyes off of God and His will, and focus on a situation, subsequently making us walk in doubt and disobedience.

> I realized that I had been depending on my own natural ability which would have been inadequate, instead of walking in faith and allowing the Holy Spirit to guide the process of writing the book. He confirmed this revelation by reminding me constantly to stay in His presence and in His Word.

I had a great experience in this area of my life. The devil struck a blow, I bowed and he took advantage of my bowing. I went down but God did not let me stay down, so, Praise God! I was up again.

When God gave me this assignment of "A Simple Man's Walk with God" I shuddered, and was afraid to share with anyone. God could not really expect me to write a book?! I do not have the ability, and thought of educated authors with degrees, so I knew for sure this could not be me. While I originally mentioned the call to my son Godfrey, it took me years to tell the second person, and I struggled with these conflicting thoughts for a long time. I even made myself believe that the devil was the one who had spoken to me and was trying to set me up to look foolish because the book would not be any good. I responded when altar calls were made to be delivered from fear, and to be enabled to fulfill my God-given assignment. I would leave those services feeling all was well. I even pondered on the scriptures about fear, yet there were no obvious changes.

Finally, I started encouraging myself in the Word. I was convinced that there was nothing more that God needed to do to ensure that I

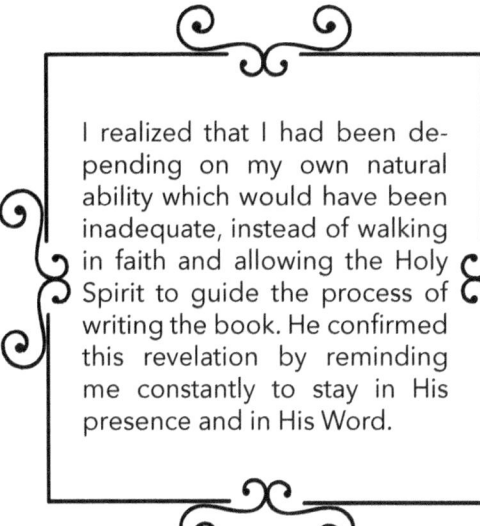

> I realized that I had been depending on my own natural ability which would have been inadequate, instead of walking in faith and allowing the Holy Spirit to guide the process of writing the book. He confirmed this revelation by reminding me constantly to stay in His presence and in His Word.

was equipped to successfully complete the task He had given me. I realized that I had been depending on my own natural ability which would have been inadequate, instead of walking in faith and allowing the Holy Spirit to guide the process of writing the book. He confirmed this revelation by reminding me constantly to stay in His presence and in His Word.

Having settled this I asked myself "Would the devil want me to write about my walk with God? Would he invite me to stay in God's presence and in His Word?" "NO!" was the resounding answer to all these questions, so then this must be God. Mind you, when God first gave me the assignment, I knew within my spirit that it was God, but if one is not vigilant enough to sustain oneself in the Word and in the presence of God, the spirit of fear can gain entry (at any time), gripping and paralyzing you, the more you dwell on the lies it presents.

The next step in my deliverance from this crippling fear was to tell a few more people about the assignment. As I did, I started receiving ideas from God and I began to write. Even with the new resolve, I could still feel fear trying to hold on. Brothers and sisters, know that fear comes directly from the throne room of the enemy who sets out to do exactly what his plan is - to steal, kill and destroy. All Praise to God as I obeyed Him, I was able to overcome that foul spirit. What first alerted me, to the fact that the fear I felt was misplaced, was the fact that normally I am not someone who is easily fearful. There must have been a weak spot and the enemy, ever ready to pounce, used it. God, however, will always have His way. He promised in His Word that all things work together for good to them that love the Lord and are called according to His purpose (Romans 8:28). He will use even this experience to help many who struggle with the spirit of fear.

While the spirit of fear exists, faith is the master tool assigned to each believer. As we study His Word, the Spirit of God will begin to operate in us, using the Word in such a way that our faith will rise. We may not understand all things, but we should believe all things of God. We may not understand the times of harvest and reaping, but God does, and we need to obey the Master and be quickened by His Spirit in order to move in His seasons.

At this time of God's outpouring of His Spirit, we cannot be fixed on traditions, or focus on what we have been accustomed to. We need to stay in tune with God. Looking upon Jesus the Author and Finisher of our faith, so that we can move when He says to move, write when He says to write, go when He says to go, and speak when He says to speak. It is His plan we are here to fulfill, and He knows all things.

> We need to stay in tune with God. Looking upon Jesus the Author and Finisher of our faith, so that we can move when He says to move, write when He says to write, go when He says to go, and speak when He says to speak. It is His plan we are here to fulfill, and He knows all things.

Daytime may have been the wrong time for fishing according to the fishermen, but the same Jesus who commands the winds and the waves, also directs the fish to where and when they should go. Jonah thought he could get away with disobeying God, but the whale was there to pick him up, swallow him and deposit him in Nineveh, the place where God had commanded him to go in the first place. He was forced to go and deliver God's message to the people, and they received it well. Did the whale have radar? Think about it.

What about when Jesus told Peter to go and get the money out of the fish to pay their taxes that were due? Peter never asked any questions; he just went. Can you imagine responding to that instruction? What would you have done?

Peter shows great faith in the Master, on the morning after not catching any fish, when Jesus asked what they had caught. These were fishermen who knew the waters. They were out all night and nothing came into the nets yet Jesus said to them, "Boys throw out your nets, go out now." Peter responds, "Master I am only doing this because you say. I will let down the nets." Peter knew this was not supposed to be the time, but he had such faith in Jesus that he went ahead and did it. The result was so great that they could not handle the catch. They sought to get help as both boats began to sink, and they were under pressure with the large catch. This is the same Jesus, in whom Peter exhibited faith, that is ours today if we dare to believe. What is our response to His call? Do we display so great a faith? Are we guided by His Holy Spirit? Are we led by His Word or do we allow the disguiser to come in and steal our joy, and peace, our rest in God and His Word? Faith brings peace and contentment and assists us to walk in obedience.

Smith Wigglesworth in one of His sermons wrote "I believe every fish in the lake tried to get into the net to see Jesus."

The disciples, experienced Jesus and Jesus said to the fishermen, "I will make you fishers of men." Matthew 4:18. If they did not respond to the Good Master would they have had such experiences to leave for us and to be able to spread the Good News? We too need to live by faith, and obey God's word, to be the testimony God created us to be, and to spread God's message to all those with whom we come into contact.

I thank God that He has strengthened my faith and my testimony through His Word so that the spirit of fear was defeated.

Loving Father on behalf of every reader, I come in agreement with You and Your Word in the Name of Jesus, taking authority over and destroying the devil's work and the spirit of fear. Help us Lord that as we study Your Word faith will arise in us, cancelling all the works of darkness and the remembrance of fear. We thank You Lord for our total deliverance in Jesus' Name. Amen.

CHAPTER FIVE

[God's Purpose Achieved Through Sacrifice]

I believe God created us in His image and likeness so that we would have His heart and be so connected to Him that His desire would burn deep inside of us until it becomes our desire.

God's desire for mankind is that none should perish, but that all should repent and have everlasting life through His son Jesus Christ. Since this is our Father's desire, if we love Him with all our heart, soul, mind and strength, this should be our desire as well. If we love our neighbour as ourselves, we should want to see each soul saved so that every person with whom we come into contact should be seen through the eyes of salvation.

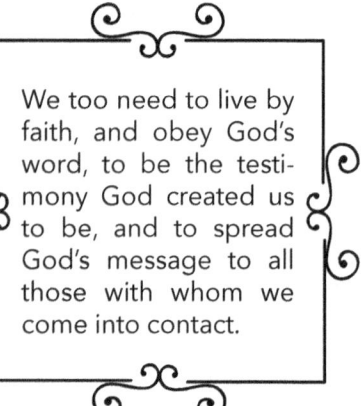

> We too need to live by faith, and obey God's word, to be the testimony God created us to be, and to spread God's message to all those with whom we come into contact.

Scripture says that God grants us the desires of our heart and if souls are really the desire of our heart, He will grant it, even when we do not see the possibility of it happening.

> *Psalm 37: 3-4; "Trust in the Lord, and do good; dwell in the land and feed on His faithfulness. Delight yourself also in the Lord, and He shall give you the desires of your heart."*

I could testify concerning God granting us desires once they are according to His will. I have a burning desire for souls, especially my family members, which extends outside my natural blood line. The Holy Spirit as the mighty teacher started teaching me how to pray for them. My prayer covers every offspring of my long gone grandparents on both sides of my family - The house of Ambrose and Gally Collins and the house of Conrad and Annette Protain - This prayer takes in all those connected by marriage or any other way and all their family members as well. I feel it is very important that we influence those connected to us with the guidance of the Lover of our souls, Jesus Christ and His Holy Spirit.

Some of my own children do not have the same belief that I have, but I believe that God will give me the desires of my heart. As recorded in the scriptures, God's completed work is done. In John 19:30 He said, "It is finished!" Therefore I know for a fact that they are already seated in heavenly places with our Lord and Saviour Jesus Christ. I know though that I must be obedient to God's Word.

> Sacrifice is hard, but it is important for the Kingdom's sake.

I already bought their Bibles as guided by the Spirit in readiness for that day. Our God is a faithful God and all things work together for good to them that love the Lord and are called according to His purpose in Romans 8:28.

Ruth, in her time of sacrifice, decided to go to a strange land with Naomi, her mother-in-law, not knowing what to expect; strange people serving a different God. She was determined to stay at Naomi's side. Ruth 1:16 — "But Ruth said: Entreat me not to leave you, or to turn back from following after you; for wherever you go, I will go; and wherever you lodge, I will lodge; your people shall be my people, and your God, my God."

Ruth's story highlights the fact that whatever God has ordained will be fulfilled, as we see in the unfolding of God's plan and purpose for Elimelech's family line. This has opened up for me a new way of thinking. If we believe that the above is true and that God is sovereign, why do we fight people and circumstances? Look at Boaz. He knew what was right and he did it. While he admired Ruth, he chose to take the chance of losing her in order to do the right thing, which was to give her first kinsman the first opportunity to redeem her.

Despite Naomi's devastating situation and the strong possibility of living out the rest of her life in loneliness and poverty, Naomi selflessly encouraged Ruth to leave her. Her selflessness was rewarded by Ruth's undying devotion to her, her people and to her God.

Did Ruth, Boaz or Naomi know that they were planting the seed of Agape (the love of God) and that by cooperating with the will of God they would be included in the direct bloodline of the Saviour?

What I see here more than anything else is the sacrifice they all made. Sacrifice is hard, but it is important for the Kingdom's sake. Blood sacrifice during the old covenant no longer exists, but we are called to present our bodies as a living sacrifice, and this is an example here for us to behold.

When we tell others about Christ, we do not know who they may become (great evangelists, apostles, prophets, pastors or teachers etc,or just a simple person who is not in the front line, but walking and fulfilling God's purpose and destiny in their life.) So we need, in our own simple way, to spread the Word. We should encourage and not pull down, share God's love and help where necessary. We will not all be chosen to be in the fore-front, but we can all be God's chosen people if we make His will our heart's desire.

We do not need to know people to show them God's Love. Let the Spirit of God guide you. God has been doing it with me and He will do it with you if you would only give Him a chance. It may be difficult at first, but with determination and God's help, you can do it.

In another scenario I went to WalMart in the USA with my son. As I entered, I came into contact with a lady who might have been in her late thirties. She was a simple looking person. She stepped back for me to pass with my trolley. While moving around the store we met again. We were not there for very long and as we were leaving we had a third encounter. In my spirit I thought "why?" We commented on the 'coincidence' of meeting three times. To me she looked like someone who had been hurt, maybe rejected and I felt led to turn around and ask her if I could give her a hug. This lady welcomed the hug and as I let her go I saw that the Lord had done something within her. She then said "Oh! I know, there are still nice people around." I saw a smile and a relaxed expression which was not there before.

Two days ago there was a funeral service for a close family member. God blessed me to travel to Punta Gorda, Florida. I believe the purpose of the trip was to close off a chapter in my family's life. I visited with my late cousin weeks before on her sick bed. It was a very trying time for all the family as well as her church family.

My cousin was a member of the prayer group at her church. During my visit I was introduced to the head of the group. She was the one responsible for organizing the program for the funeral. After the funeral service, I met her in the corridor and said hello. She was trying to get into a room really quickly and somehow I felt (I know it was the leading of the Lord) that I needed to get to her and so I did just that. As I got her attention I said to her "Let me give you a hug" and that is when I realized she was retreating into the room to burst into tears. She was disappointed with a little flaw in the program that really amounted to nothing. Her response was to thank me and to say that she could always benefit from a hug, and I felt her body relax.

When God spreads His Love through us, we need to respond and let Him have His way. Our Apostle, Pastor and other Ministers, have been teaching us by their preaching and by their living examples how to love. Not too long ago we received a message on how someone received deliverance through a hug after having been prayed for several times.

> Our love must cost. Ruth's love for Naomi cost her everything that mattered at that time and through her sacrifice, her gain far exceeded anything that she lost.

As we love the way God commanded us to love, which is to love the Lord our God and to love our neighbor as ourselves, we will see the hand of God move mightily on the earth. Our love must cost. Ruth's love for Naomi cost her everything that mattered at that time and through her sacrifice, her gain far exceeded anything that she lost.

Any offering to God must cost as King David said in 2 Samuel 24:24:

But the king replied to Araunah, "No, I insist on paying you for it. I will not sacrifice to the LORD my God burnt offerings that cost me nothing."

Certain decisions are never easy to make and may cost us our friends and resources, and cause heartache. When Jesus suffered and died on the Cross it was far from easy, but because the gift of His death and suffering would lead to our eternal life He felt it was truly worth it. What are you willing to give up for the advancement of the Kingdom of God?

For me, one of the sacrifices I had to make, in obedience to God, caused me to be put in a very interesting position in my former home church. This is the denomination in which I had grown up, and was encouraged to use my talents wisely. I enjoyed what I was called to do, and God started guiding me in many new areas. I started hearing directions from God that were different from the norm. I did not fully understand, so I procrastinated, and delayed the process somewhat, but nevertheless I obeyed. Never for one moment did I realize that I was being prepared for a big move which was going to cost me.

Moving involves a condition of the heart. We must decide what we are prepared to give up. If we do not we will suffer the fate Lot's wife suffered. After not making a clean break with Sodom, she could not resist looking back at what she was meant to totally leave, which resulted in her turning into a pillar of salt. Ruth's sister-in-law Orpah knew what she could handle, so she took Naomi's advice and left, however, Ruth felt she would pay the price to stay with her mother in law, no matter what the cost.

Reflecting on my move, which was very difficult, I recognized it was a God ordained move. It could have been harmful though, if my response was different. I know that the Grace of God was at work to protect my walk with Him and I am truly thankful. The situation was somewhat embarrassing and my reputation could have been challenged. I was given a direction by my Lord, which was contrary to the church's doctrine and when I responded I was immediately released from all leadership positions. I was told that the only way I could be restored was if I repented for obeying what the Lord required of me. To me this was not an option, and while I was sad, I am truly happy to say that I have benefited so much from that move. My experiences and spiritual growth has surely been of considerable help to so many people, that God would bring across my path. I pray that the Kingdom of God has benefited as well.

God said, 'I will build My Church, and the gates of Hades shall not prevail against it. "Matthew 16:18. God knew what He wanted to achieve in me, and He did what needed to be done to accomplish what He wanted.

There has never been a time that I have had to sacrifice some thing for God and not subsequently see a mighty move of God. Many times I would make a decision to give up something that I wanted to do, in order to help someone else, and I would see such a beautiful assignment for the Lord flow out of it.

Jesus was our sacrifice. We too must live a joyful, happy life of sacrifice unto Him. There are great and mighty benefits for us and our generations to come. Someone must sacrifice for someone else to gain. The world is awaiting our sacrifice, for the sons of God to arise and shine.

Lord and Saviour show us the way that You have called us to walk, so that we can walk in truth. Help us to recognize that even though blood sacrifice has ended, we are called to be a living sacrifice for You. You are our Lord and Master, keep us in Your presence always and let Your Holy Spirit dwell in us always. In Jesus' Name. Amen.

CHAPTER SIX

[A Book of Remembrance]

I really, really do love remembrances. It has been tremendously helpful in my walk with my Lord, as I was able to reflect on God's goodness either to me or someone else. And I believe much honour is due to this book of remembrance- The BIBLE. God has made it so that we have His Word for us to experience and some of His works which tell of His goodness, trials and tests, while reminding us that He is the same God of yesterday, today and forever. Whatever we need can be found in this great book; testimonies, teachings, guidance and more than enough food for a life time.

For example, here is some food that has blessed me.
(1) Malachi 3:16-18 Beautiful Jewels made for God.

"Then those who feared the Lord spoke to one another, and the Lord listened and heard them. So a book of remembrance was written before Him for those who fear the Lord and who meditate on His Name. 'They shall be mine,' says the Lord of hosts, "on the day that I make them My jewels and I will spare them as a man spares his own son who serves him.' Then you shall again discern between the righteous and the wicked, between one who serves God and one who does not serve Him.

This scripture tells us that God wants a people who fear Him, true worshippers, a people unto Himself, those who will not complain or grumble but will praise Him in the midst of adversity. We were created by Almighty God to be His presence on the earth, and as such we are called to show forth all of God's qualities as we live our lives. In this light we must think seriously as we speak, act, and respond recognizing that Jesus is in our midst always. In other words we are called to be Ambassadors showing forth Christ's integrity. Then God will make us His Jewels. I feel strongly that God wants us to have a book of remembrance as individuals, families, communities, nations and most of all His Church.

As we read these verses one should recognize God as our great and awesome God, a Father above Fathers who is concerned about His children and listens to us at all times, even when we are not speaking to Him. In the previous scripture verse, our Abba (Father) was eavesdropping on His children. He recognizes those who fear Him as His children. "Then those who feared the Lord spoke to one another", they were talking among themselves, but God who is everywhere can hear even when we think. He made it His business to hear, and what He heard being of great importance to Him, He received and used for His Glory.

"So a book of remembrance was written before Him for those who fear the Lord and who meditate on His name." Also Malachi 4:2 tells us; "But to you who fear My name-The Sun of Righteousness shall arise with healing in His wings;" The other verses give us even more promises of victory.

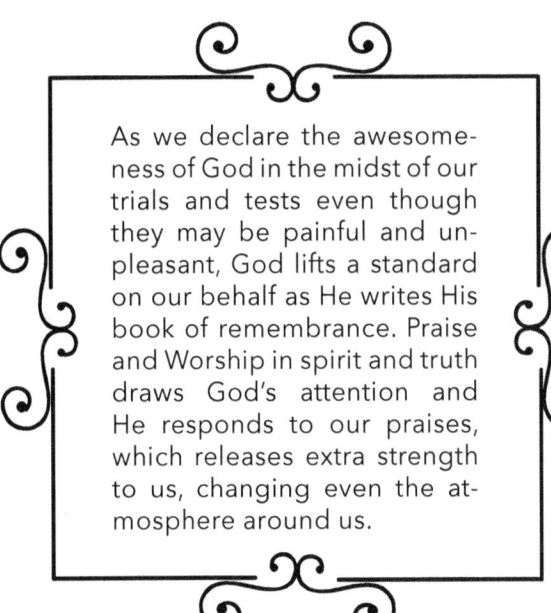

As we declare the awesomeness of God in the midst of our trials and tests even though they may be painful and unpleasant, God lifts a standard on our behalf as He writes His book of remembrance. Praise and Worship in spirit and truth draws God's attention and He responds to our praises, which releases extra strength to us, changing even the atmosphere around us.

How great is our God! A great and mighty God who takes His children seriously while testifying and lifting up the name of Jesus as we proclaim, "Look at what the Lord has done." As we declare the awesomeness of God in the midst of our trials and tests even though they may be painful and unpleasant, God lifts a standard on our behalf as He writes His book of remembrance. Praise and Worship in spirit and truth draws God's attention and He responds to our praises, which releases extra strength to us, changing even the atmosphere around us.

Hallelujah!! Praise His Holy Name!!!
We must never be quiet about what God has done. It is important for us to record and share our experiences. Even though they may be insignificant to us, we never know when someone would benefit greatly from them. Another reason for us to practice sharing is that as we share, and lift up the Name of Jesus, He is exalted. He then draws all men unto Himself and the devil is defeated. The word of our testimony encourages others. The weak becomes stronger and we become bolder, overcoming fear to speak as we purposefully engage spreading His love.

In Malachi 3:17, says, "They shall be Mine," says the Lord of hosts, "On the day that I make them My jewels. And I will spare them As a man spares His own son who serves him." I love this verse, it is so wonderful to know that God puts His stamp upon these people; a stamp of ownership. When I think of God calling me His jewel; His special treasure, it truly humbles me and has a great impact on the way I represent Him!

God not only honours, but He equates us to a son who serves a father. Jesus served His Father honourably and being our example, we must make sure to serve our Father in like manner, so that we too can be lights for the Kingdom of God.

REMEMBRANCE IN SERVICE.

Service is one of the hallmarks of Christianity. In Matthew 20: 20-28, Jesus was setting things in order. There was a question about who would be the greatest and sit at His right hand and at His left hand in the Kingdom. A mother on her knees requested these positions for her sons, but Jesus never encouraged that type of activity. He distinctly showed the difference between the world and the church. He made it clear that to even be considered for greatness, you must be a servant first.

True service can only be accomplished through love for God and the love of God. As we truly accept Jesus Christ as Lord, we become co-heirs with Him and agape, the God kind of love, begins to fill our heart. The more we grow in His love, the greater our

service for the Kingdom becomes.
While at the last supper, Jesus took off his outer garment, placed a towel around Him, poured water, and washed the disciples' feet. He surely left us with perfect examples, exhibiting humility.

Even after His resurrection while the disciples were out fishing, their Lord and Master prepared a meal and set the table for them to sup with Him. What an example we have to follow; Jesus, Son of man, Son of God, a servant of His Father as well as of His brethren. His entire life exemplified service. As a matter of fact, He is still serving, "at the right hand of God," as our Divine Intercessor.

As co- heirs with Jesus, we are called to serve our beloved Father. If we expect to follow in this great legacy of love that Jesus left us, we must adhere to His Word. John 14: 15 "If you love me, keep my commandment." John 14:23 reminds us of the promise, "If anyone loves Me he will keep My word; and My Father will love him, and We will come to him and make Our home with him." These examples were left for us in the scriptures as remembrances that we are to follow. God's love is so amazing that Jesus left us with the privilege and honour to have the Holy Spirit dwelling in every believer empowering us with power and might. He has unlimited power.

REMEMBRANCES AS MEMORIALS

Remembrances are considered memorials and established in different ways. God told the children of Israel to build memorials as highlights of their journey, so that when their children saw and asked, they could teach them about God's goodness. This would encourage the children to pass on their experiences with God from generation to generation, giving them a true life picture of what it means to walk with Him. Also reminding them that no matter what they go through, God should always be of prime importance in their lives. This is still necessary in our day to fulfill God's purpose and His Plan.

I believe we have strayed from this teaching and need to get back to that practice. Pride or an honest desire to protect our children from the unpleasant, prevents us from seeing the importance of teaching them how God stands up on our behalf and guides us through our difficult times as well as good times.

We have to consciously determine in our minds to teach the children about our trials and tests. If not, they will believe things were always easy for us, and when they face a challenge or obstacle they may fall apart, thinking life is not fair, or "why me?"

When we don't teach them, we leave them without ammunition to fight, nothing to reflect on, no memories of seeing parents or elders go through and come out victorious, no battles fought on their knees or in a prayer closet. What about the testimonies given during our Worship service? What are our remembrances?

I have found, as I build a memorial to the Lord, it forces me to remember His goodness, even when it comes through difficult times. Fiery trials do wonders for our perfecting if we receive them with joy. There is great benefit in hardship. It draws people together as long as Jesus is allowed to have HIS way in grooming us.

> Fiery trials do wonders for our perfecting if we receive them with joy. There is great benefit in hardship. It draws people together once Jesus is allowed to have HIS way in grooming us.

As I look back I bless the Lord for all that I have been through. My experiences have strengthened me to stand and be a testimony for God. I am able to be God's arms of compassion to someone who is in need of a helping hand. It also enables others to get some comfort knowing that they are not alone and that someone else went through similar situations and overcame.

At the time of the hardship, certainly it is not joyful. Sometimes you feel you want to die, but God's grace and His favour often overtake us, and as we meditate on God's Word we can rise to praise Him in the midst. I remember times when in the midst of my trials, joy came out of nowhere and I strongly believe that someone, somewhere was praying on my behalf. There are times you may encounter someone in a much worse position than you. The experience awakens you, shaking you to reality out of your 'major' trouble as you realize it to be minor.

REMEMBRANCES IN OUR DAILY WALK:

Remembrances are built through our daily walk with the Master. Whether good, bad or indifferent, we can see God's faithfulness in the eyes of adversity. As we believe Romans 8:28, that all things work together for good to those who love God, to those who are called according to His purpose. As the goodness unfolds, we can then value those around us as well as the perfection of God's plan. It is important for us to value God the Father, the Son Jesus, and the precious Holy Spirit, who leads us into remembrances.
Remembrances are built in service to God, so as we serve Him in our daily walk, experiences of all types will come. They may knock us down but not out, and all these will be of great value to people around us as we move on and up. Remembrances will live on long after we are gone.

As we build our remembrances we must keep our relationship and our eyes focused on the Father like Jesus did. He never took His eyes off His Father. When we lose our focus we are hindered, and will not resume until we come back into full relationship. It takes a right heart condition to keep building.

As we build memorials or remembrances to God, we weaken the enemy and he loses power in our lives. When we do this and can see our trials as stepping stones to victory, we become more than conquerors.

One of my major remembrances goes back twenty-three years. What could easily have resulted in my physical or spiritual death, and potentially destroy an entire family, was really a stepping stone to a higher level in the Lord.

> God not only preserved me but had me focus on this child who murdered my son, enabling me to lift him up in prayer, asking God for his salvation, deliverance and peace.

My precious, first born son, Nikita, on the threshold of manhood, at 19 was savagely murdered by a 15 year old. My first thought was that the perpetrator was only a babe; the age of my fourth son! Even in the intense pain at the loss of my son, my heart really went out to this child wondering what could cause him to commit such an offense without any aggravation. Most mothers in this situation, especially single mothers as I was, would have fallen apart. I know of some who became bitter, and lost in unforgiveness, and certainly would have given up on God who might have appeared to them to be absent and uncaring. There was concern by family and friends, about the possibility of my having a breakdown, but by God's divine intervention I was kept. God not only preserved me but had me focus on this child who murdered my son, enabling me to lift him up in prayer, asking God for his salvation, deliverance and peace.

I did not know at the time that a Remembrance was being built. I only became aware of it when God led me to write this chapter.

> Given my experience, I am more equipped to bear the burden for restoration, to mobilize a community of prayer warriors and to apply the healing balm to the mothers and words of wisdom and exhortation to the sons who are exposed to this life of death.

He remains on my prayer list as in faith I believe God for the finished work. Even if I don't see him on the earth, I am sure I will see him in heaven. Presently, as God would have it, I have been living in a literal warzone, in which frequently, more mothers (parents) are losing their sons to acts of violence as they are blindly falling prey to the false honour of wearing a criminal's hat. Given my experience, I am more equipped to bear the burden for restoration, to mobilize a community of prayer warriors and to apply the healing balm to the mothers and words of wisdom and exhortation to the sons who are exposed to this life of death.

My prayer to Almighty God and Father is that we would honour Him for who He is and that we would come to appreciate all that He has done for us and has given to us; that we would accept Him as our Lord and Saviour, so that we can build strong remembrances for His Glory, destroying all forces that would prevent us from doing so. I pray that our remembrances would overtake all facets of worldly remembrances. Father we exalt Jesus Christ as Lord and Saviour with thanksgiving in our hearts, in the precious name of Jesus the Christ, the only true and living God. Amen

CHAPTER SEVEN

[God's Perfect Plan: God Loves Agreement]
PART ONE

God's completed work was done before the beginning of time. I can truly say from my experiences that God's plan for our lives is perfect. It would be nice to have blue prints. I am sure they exist, however, God often orchestrates things in such a way that they are completely outside of our control.

Many years ago, I frequently visited Tobago for a number of different reasons. (Trinidad and Tobago is a twin Island State). Then for quite a long time I did not set foot on Tobago. In 2002 I started feeling a pull in my spirit to visit the island, "but why" I asked? No answer came. I ignored the stirring but the feeling that I should go, never left. Was it for a rest, change of atmosphere? Then suddenly something happened on the inside of me, just a, I know that I know, and that enabled me to make a decision and I was sure then that I needed to go to Tobago. Election was soon to be held in Tobago around that time as well, and this would have been a deterrent for me, at that time really. I later got confirmation about my trip.

One day while speaking to one of my spiritual daughters who was born and bred in Tobago, I mentioned to her what was happening and she said to me, "You know Mummy will be happy to have you. When do you want to go? Just tell me and you organize". Her response was so quick that I was lost for words. I organized and was shortly on my way.

Indeed her mum was glad! We had known each other for a number of years. Her grandson is also my God given grandson. What we did not know at that time was that God had a plan. I went for a few days and ended up staying a week.

God often deposits ideas and thoughts deep into your spirit when He wants you to play a role in fulfilling a specific purpose. Many times I cannot tell you that I would hear an audible voice, but I would feel a great desire to do this or that, or to go here or there. This was one of those occasions.

I got to Tobago and felt very much at home. I just let God have His way. We chatted a lot, shared experiences, read the Word together, prayed and listened to what God was saying. We relaxed and enjoyed each other's company. I did not have any knowledge of her family history, but as we fellowshipped God started doing something, showing me some areas where there was some hurt and where prayer support and agreement were needed. God had prepared her for this time when many deep seated issues would be addressed. These areas included the desires of her heart and so she willingly cooperated with me as I followed God's lead in the matter.

We followed the guidance of the Holy Spirit, we prayed, rededicated the home, blessed and declared the home holy ground for God's Kingdom.

As mothers and grandmothers we prayed for our children and grandchildren. She lived alone; a very strong lady taking care of her home and yard. The time spent was very pleasant. We bonded a great deal more and a beautiful relationship blossomed. We did what God set before us and He took charge. We prayed and God answered according to His plan. We did not understand at the time what God was about to do. The very first evidence of answered prayer was her son moving back to the home to live with her. She was very surprised by this action. God however, was not surprised because He was getting ready to take her home to be with Him, and wanted to give both of them an opportunity to spend time together.

One fine afternoon, the son had plans to go to a football match but then decided not to go. He was at home when his mother needed him, and was able to take her to the hospital. She was experiencing pain but did not suspect a heart attack. Before the doctors were finished attending to her, she was taken home to be with the Lord.

God healed, restored, transformed and set things on course for her to be at peace before taking her home. Because of His compassion and love, He did not allow her to die alone in the house.

PART TWO

One morning after praying I heard an audible voice telling me to call one of my daughters. I did not know why I should call but had learnt by then that as I obeyed, God's plan would be revealed. So I called her early that morning and after the pleasantries, I immediately found myself asking, "What do you want from your children's dad? " Her reply was "Aunty Jan, for us to get married". I replied, "but you must need something else before that, what about salvation? She replied, "Oh yes Aunty Jan, sure, sure, that must be first." So I explained what had happened and that I needed to come in agreement with her for what she wanted.

This situation was an example of the greatest works of Almighty God who for many years had worked on the hearts of these two people helping them to love each other with a pure heart while they waited on God. This lady deserves a medal for patience and the gentleman for fortitude.

We agreed in prayer for his salvation and for the marriage and in a matter of months, one night when I was assisting at the altar, I felt the Holy Spirit turn my head to the right only to behold this very son at the altar surrendering his life to the Lord. They were married months later. God be praised for the manner in which He moved in their situation. They have two grown sons and had lived together for several years. When she accepted the Lord, she continued to live in the house but sought to be celibate (not to have sexual relations with him) as she desired to honour God. During that season of their lives they prayed together and he covered his family. He was and still is a peach of a gentleman and she, a woman of virtue.

In the two above scenarios, we are reminded that God loves agreement, while the devil gloats in separation. We must prove him a liar.

Father help us, Lord God to see Your very heart and how much You require us to be united and to be in agreement, so that as we walk in love united and agreeing that we will see Your Kingdom come and Your will be done on earth as it is in heaven. Father we know this can only happen in the name of Jesus Christ and in His love. Thank You Oh Lord for giving us the power of agreement. Help us Lord to understand that You love us, and You need us to be led by Your Holy Spirit always, so that we will be able to truly serve You as You require us to do, and fulfill purpose and destiny in Jesus Name. Amen.

CHAPTER EIGHT

[Trip to Texas]

The highlight of this particular trip to Washington D.C. was the graduation of Natalie, my daughter-in- Christ, my son's wife. Her parents, family members and friends all came together for the double celebration of her completion of Law School and her birthday.

After the graduation, we had an extensive trip planned. The plan was that we would drive to Orlando to my great niece's graduation, spend a few days with them, then go on to my brother's home in Coral Springs, Florida. My son and his wife would go on a cruise, while I visited with my brother and family until their return. We would then return to Orlando where I would meet with family to go on to Atlanta, while they returned to their home in Washington D.C.

This was our plan, but shortly after the grand celebration, we learned that Natalie's grandfather had suddenly passed on. As a result of the news, the focus changed and they started making arrangements to go to Texas for the funeral. They suggested that I still travel to Orlando for the graduation. At first I thought this would be okay, but later I felt that I shouldn't go as my spirit was not at peace with this plan. I believed that at this time of bereavement, I needed to be supportive, so I decided I would join them on the trip to Texas for the funeral. As I did, my spirit settled, and I was at peace.

We drove to Atlanta and then on to Texas, getting there two days before the funeral. It was necessary, however, for us to leave the evening after the funeral in order to be in Florida in time for them to go on the cruise.

When we got to San Antonio, TX, I realized that there was some mild competition between two sisters in the family regarding who would host me. This I thought to be amusing. At the wedding two years prior, I met these family members and we bonded well. The older sister pulled rank using her seniority and the younger sister gave way, so I was accommodated by her.

We were all on the way to the house and my hostess said something that I did not quite understand until later on. She had a situation at her house that required nothing less than God's intervention. We got to the house and there was a spirit of heaviness. I did not know what was happening then. I was shown to my room and there was a beautiful little baby asleep. I do not even remember who else I saw at that time. I was very tired and wanted more than anything to sleep, which I did.

In the morning I awoke and all seemed well. I got dressed. When I got out of the room I saw an entire family, two children of school age, the baby that I saw in the room and their mum, (who is the mother of all three children), the other adult was the children's maternal grandmother. Natalie's aunt had graciously put this family up for the last two years.

I felt drawn to the two school children. I spoke with them for a while before they left for school. It was an opportunity to tell them about Jesus, and how much He loves them. They were happy about the time I spent with them, and did not seem to be in a hurry to go to school.

The grandmother looked after the baby while the mother went to work for a few hours, but she appeared not to be capable of looking after herself, much less a baby. I was led to tell the grandmother about God and His greatness, His love, and what we can do in His strength. God just took charge as I started talking to her. Her solace seemed to be in the cigarette. She smoked like a chimney, and had no drive or real desire for anything. I encouraged her to get into a relationship with Jesus. She received all that I said and then started telling me what was happening. I realized she had hit a hard place, and that she did not have the strength to continue fighting. She just kept going under. God was ready to have her move out of that state of hopelessness and into a higher level in Him, and she did. I led her in the sinner's prayer as she committed her life to Jesus. Immediately I saw heaviness lift off of her and some light flood over her and she started seeing things differently.

The report that I received later on was that the things that seemed so difficult to get going, all started falling into place, and there was great improvement. She was scheduled to get an apartment, and assistance to help them get back on track. I am sure she and her family are now in a much better position.

In her heart she must have prayed, and her friend who assisted her by giving her a helping hand and allowing them to stay at her home, must have been praying as well. Sometimes things are more readily received from a stranger, who may be saying the same thing, but it is received differently. Love shown through a vessel of God is always victorious and destroys many strongholds. Not only was I able to be supportive of my son's wife and her family, but I was able to minister to the family whom God had waiting for me. Whatever it may take, God always knows. He makes sure that He answers in a time He allots, which is the perfect time. Praise God!

This grandmother is now a Deaconess in the Church. See what God can do. If He did it for her, He can do it for you. Nothing is too difficult for our God.

Precious Father, You are our only hope. Without You we are at a place where we will not know where to turn, and what to do. Thank You for Your Holy Spirit who is with us to be our help when we need Him. It is such a privilege to be able to look to You in our time of need, and to know that You are waiting for us with open arms. Help us Holy Spirit to be quickened at all times to move as the Father requires us to, so that we can fulfill God's mighty plan. Thank You for your faithfulness always, in Jesus name. Amen.

CHAPTER NINE

[Our Expectations vs. God's Plan]

I must be about my Father's business". Jesus knew exactly what His mission was about. When his parents were looking for Him after the Feast of the Passover, Jesus was just 12 years old. Luke 2: 48-50 – "So when they saw Him, they were amazed; and His mother said to Him, "Son why have You done this to us? Look, Your father and I have sought You anxiously." And He said to them, "Why did you seek Me? Did you not know that I must be about My Father's business?" But they did not understand this statement which He spoke to them. Was it that Mary did not understand why this perfect child would stray away from them or was it that her expectations were different from God's plan?

Jesus came to earth in the flesh to fulfill God's purpose and plan, to redeem us from sin so that we could be restored to our rightful position- God's image and likeness as beautifully and powerfully described in His Word.

In John 1:1-16 Jesus is highlighted here showing that He came to earth to reveal and declare to us the full picture of our heavenly Father,- His Glory , His Grace, His Truth and His Love. The WORD that was from the beginning, this same WORD was with GOD and was GOD, became flesh and dwelt among us. This WORD is JESUS.

The Father used John the Baptist, Jesus' cousin, to prepare the way for the people to accept Jesus for who He was in His fullness.

John the Baptist and his Lord Jesus' first encounter occurred when their mothers greeted each other. It was a miraculous moment when John in Elizabeth's womb, leapt for joy in response to the recognition of Jesus while he too was in His mother Mary's womb. As their mothers greeted each other, John responded to His Lord, as recorded in scripture: (Luke 1:26-45). John was sent to bear witness to the Light, the true Light that gives light to every man coming into the world.

God has made provision for us to receive that Light, but the choice is ours. God's plan, as our Father, is perfect because he has groomed us even to the point of the families into which we were born. As parents, we map out a course for our children as we feel it should be, or as society expects. However, our expectations can be very different from God's, as is seen in many cases. It is mostly done with good intentions. We believe maturity and experience give us clearer vision, so we see things differently, and children feel they know for sure what is best for them. When parents at that point step back, their sons and daughters usually return to the place of reason.

I had to keep reminding myself with my own children that while in my own human understanding I might have wanted certain things for them, God had a plan and HIS Plan will always prevail. We have lots of examples, i.e., the prodigal son, the Israelites, and in closer proximity, we ourselves. We bounce about, take some knocks, and then come to our senses. God allows us to choose knowing full well that our heart condition will eventually respond to His bidding, and we will return to fulfill His purpose and destiny.

It is important for us to study GOD's Word, teach our children, and encourage those around us as well so that the Word will become alive in us. We must believe that no matter what we may see or how it may look to us, God is faithful to complete the work started in us, Romans 9:28.

While I was visiting with my son Godfrey in Washington D.C. a few years ago, I received a phone call that my brother in London was not doing well. I knew he was diagnosed with prostate cancer a few years before, but he seemed to be okay. I made contact and he sounded very strong. This was misleading based on the information I had received, so I checked with his companion. She confirmed that he was weakening rapidly, and that the strength in his voice was deceptive. My son and I prayed and discussed the possibility of my going to visit him.

This decision would be dependent on a few things. My return ticket to Trinidad would expire in about a week's time and this surely would not give me much time. Yet if I went home, the cost of a return ticket would be out of my reach. I contacted my Pastor who told me I should go to London and make sure all was well with him. I understood just what he meant.

With that in mind, I decided (or thought I decided) to call the airline to check the possibility of getting an extension on the ticket. To me, this seemed crazy but it was just a phone call and worth a try. I did make the call and the answer was negative. It looked hopeless.

I love challenges at times, so I told my son what the response was, and asked him to agree with me in prayer as I intended to call again tomorrow. We agreed in prayer, trusting God would make a way where there seemed to be no way.

Very early the next morning I was on the phone requesting to speak to a Supervisor. I was asked "In connection with what matter?" As I explained my dilemma, the voice on the line asked me to please hold. On her return, I was asked a few questions and again, she asked me to hold a while longer. I was asking for a week in addition to the few days that I had, thinking I will not push for too long a period, as it might result in a refusal of my request.

When she returned to the phone, I could hardly believe what I was hearing. I got an extension of 1 [one] month! I then braced myself for the cost, only to find out that there was no extra cost to my originally discounted ticket! This was definitely a Blessing from Almighty GOD and for HIS KINGDOM's purpose. I had to get verification from his doctor in London stating his condition and prognosis, which I was able to get barring a few constraints, the difference in time being a major one, and also a hitch with the fax machine.

Things just fell into place. I was excited to see how God and God alone was unfolding His plan. God was showing Himself strong as always! There was a deadline to meet in order to expedite this new arrangement. All this information had to be in the system at the airport before the expiration of the ticket. I met the deadline and I praised and thanked God since He alone was able to get this done.

While this process was ongoing, Godfrey was checking airfares. We were certainly amazed by the price of the tickets. This was God ordained. I handed every part of this trip over to my Abba, knowing that as He took charge, things ran smoothly. I paid a price for my ticket from the US to London, that was much less than from one state to another in the USA.

My dear brother, Walter, perked up somewhat after hearing that I was on my way to visit him, but he thought that I would be with him for a week or so. Joy was written all over his face when he asked when I was leaving and I responded in 3 weeks' time! With a big smile on his face, he ordered his first meal telling them to give me charge of the kitchen. He really felt he could eat and gain back his strength to be up again, I felt so as well.

I felt God would raise him up, even though I was told the cancer had spread to the bones. I was not perturbed at all, for with God all things are possible when situations appear to be impossible. God was setting the stage to ensure that He alone would get the glory when those situations were resolved.

I did not believe the doctor's report!

I prepared the meal he requested and he ate, although not as much as he felt he could eat. This continued for a few days. He did a few things that he had not done in a while such as coming downstairs, but the improvement was short lived. He experienced much pain and this weakened him tremendously.

During my stay which was really focused on him, I wanted to make sure that I was in tune with the Holy Spirit and I was doing what God wanted. I knew that I needed to make sure he committed his life to God and that all was well with his soul. As I prayed, I felt he was healed, so no matter what I saw in the physical, my faith in what God would do was not challenged.

There was a young brother from our congregation in Trinidad and Tobago who resided in London at that time. He was very close to my brother and so Walter called him and told him that I was there. He did come by and was surprised to see his condition. He was speaking to my brother all the time over the phone, but because he was still sounding so very strong, there was no indication that he was so ill. The faithfulness of this young brother, Rozano, was amazing. The only place that I wanted to be able to go while there was to Worship Service. I was truly thankful to him because he committed to take me to the services and was there to pick me up every time there was one.

This congregation became my church family. They exhibited all godly principles, and Evangelist Lawrence Oji, affectionately known as Brother Solution, answered our call when needed and checked on us even when there was no request. He is truly a man with a heart for God and a spirit that never gives up on anyone. In keeping with his mighty testimony, he says if God never gave up on him, he could not give up on anyone.

Shortly after I got there, within the first few days, my brother committed his life to the Lord and for the remainder of my stay there, he would ask me to play Praise CD's that I brought with me. His focus was on the things of God. If he was not listening to the music, he would have me read the scriptures or pray with him. We would talk at times about things he remembered, people he wanted to see, and things he planned to do. His condition was going downhill. I saw it in the physical, yet he was getting stronger spiritually and I 'knew' that he would totally recover. I knew it and he himself declared his healing. Meanwhile the pain actually took over his entire body, and his movement was reduced greatly.

I had an expectation or I should say we had an expectation, and our expectation was based on God's Word "By whose stripes you were healed" 1 Peter 2:24; "And by His stripes we are healed" Isaiah 53: 5 and a statement that my brother made to GOD, " God I am ready to go to the Jews, to tell them the truth." You see he lived in a Jewish community, and he spoke with most of them. He was one of the few non-Jews who lived in this area, and they embraced him warmly. I was sure that he too knew that he would rise up from the sick bed and I felt sure that God would raise him up and he would become an integral part of evangelizing this community.

God's ways are beyond our comprehension. He works in ways that are just well planned and marvelous.

My brother was so overwhelmed with pain yet he made decisions that helped everyone. He did not want to be hospitalized, but he

was aware of his condition and knew that I would be leaving, and until things got better he would not be able to help himself.
Knowing that after I left, his companion would be left alone with him, he decided, two days before my departure, that he would go to the hospital for a while to ease the situation. He was admitted the day before I left.

I knew when I left that all was well with his soul and I looked forward to a call that he was cancer free. His spirit was certainly free, and he was ready to go forth with a mighty testimony. Where to? THE JEWS! This was his heart's desire, and knowing God gives us the desires of our heart, I actually saw this community transformed for Jesus. To this day, I can see the completed work there. During my visit, I prayer walked the area and claimed it for Jesus. The presence of God is released in the community and God is at work.
I visited him on my way to the airport and kept in touch over the phone until they sedated him so highly that it became difficult. He was moved to the Hospice, and they prepared everyone that it was just a matter of a few days. In all of this I still felt God was at work and yes He was at work; just not how I expected.

Finally I got a call saying that his physical body could no longer carry him. He was called home. Not for one moment do I want you to believe that healing did not take place! I believe he was healed. Healing takes place in different ways. My brother Walter was healed. God chooses how healing takes place and HE did it His way. He always knows the result He wants to accomplish.

"He was so much at peace". This was the testimony of the Chaplain that I saw a few weeks after his death. "He surely did something to me. I am sorry that I did not know him when he was stronger." He is remembered by the nurses, the doctors, patients and long after by his Jewish neighbours who still talk about him. Those who did not know he passed on would come to ask about him because they were not seeing him. They told us how much they enjoyed chatting with him when he would walk the dog, or go to buy papers.

I had an expectation, like most of you could bear witness to, but God's plan is the only truth. He holds the future and knows what is best for us and certainly GOD's priority is HIS KINGDOM. He deals with us in regard to His Kingdom. When the Kingdom of God prospers through us we prosper. Many times we have to sacrifice for the

Kingdom of God, but we must remember the sacrifice that God's Son made for us, and God says "I am with you always". So as we sacrifice He is there with us. "I will never leave you nor forsake you."

From my experiences, I have come to realize that even if I have expectations, I must truly trust God, release those expectations to Him and free myself to receive His divine plan. This is vital for us as God's plan is accomplished in our lives. Even while I had my expectations, I was prepared for whatever God was doing, if not I could have been shaken by the outcome.

I pray that this will help someone. In our limited capacity to understand, we have our expectations, but our expectations do not always match or fit into God's plan. We must be reminded that God's plan is perfect. He is a perfect God and there are no flaws in Him or His plan. As I reflect over the years, I can see God's faithfulness flows through and into His plan for His Kingdom's sake.

May His Kingdom come and His Will be done in my life and yours even as you read.

I have learned so much in situations like these. When I read the scriptures and see the words on the pages come alive, it is for me a frightening, but awesome time.

It is necessary for us to allow the scriptures to become practical for us. Knowing the scriptures is not enough. We can know the Word and even recite it, but not put it into practice. I believe we lack here.

God says, "Be anxious for nothing, but in prayer and supplication, with thanksgiving, let your request be made known to God; and the peace of God, which surpasses all understanding will guard your hearts and minds through Christ Jesus" (Philippians 4:6). My experience has been that the peace of God comes in and fills you to overflowing in that time of need and that Peace matures to a beautiful REST in God when you know that all is well.

"All things work together for good to them that love the Lord and are called according to His purpose in Christ Jesus."

May the Peace of God be with you always.

CHAPTER TEN

[We are God's Workmanship]

GOD created us with purpose and destiny in mind. He formed us in a unique pattern, crafted, moulded and fitted for His Glory.

Love makes a big difference in how we do and see things. Since God is Love, this was reflected in God's creation of man. He had a master piece in mind, but man did not understand the workmanship of God and felt he could do better, but failed. A disappointment to God; but God knew He was going to rectify this through His one and only son Jesus Christ, by sending Him to earth to teach us some important lessons first, then by having Him suffer and die, shed His blood to redeem, cleanse and purify us, so that we would look and feel like God's workmanship again. God has not failed, we failed. Are we going to fail again, or are we going to show forth God's Glory via His workmanship?

The Potter is here to fashion a people to walk in the footsteps of Jesus; footsteps of love, faith, obedience and submission to the Father's will.
When God created the earth He looked at His work and said it was good. His awesomeness and beauty are shown forth in all that He does. God is a God of divine order. Everything is well planned and timed, with precise directions. You are not left guessing.

Revelations 3: 7, "And to the angel of the church in Philadelphia write, These things says He who is holy, He who is true, He who has the key of David, He who opens and no one shuts, and shuts and no one opens.

Brother Noah was chosen by God to build the ark. He believed what God said to him and followed all the directions given to him. There is no record of Noah questioning these instructions. After reading this report a number of times, one day it suddenly occurred to me, "Where was the lock for the door?" Did God forget the lock? No! He took the responsibility of locking and opening the door Himself. God knows that when He shuts a door no man can open it, and when He opens a door no man can shut it.

Those people that surrounded Noah had ample time to heed what Noah was saying. He preached the Word of God for many years, but no one listened. As a matter of fact while he was building the ark, they made much fun of him. This never deterred Noah. He kept focused on God's call on his life. God fashioned Noah for this purpose. While he walked in obedience, God knew his heart, and knew that when the rain started and the water started rising, people would get scared and start running to the ark seeking refuge. In his humanity Noah would have responded to their cries and in so doing go contrary to God's will, therefore God protected Noah's purpose by relieving him of the responsibility by shutting the door Himself.

Every second of the day God is teaching His children something. Whatever we do has a learning experience attached, either for the present or the future, and certainly for use in His kingdom.

When God places us somewhere, it is

> When God places us somewhere, it is always for a divine purpose. He may place us in a job that we may not like. In situations like this we tend to show our discontent by fretting or refusing to put forth our best. However, we must be mindful that as vessels in preparation for Kingdom use, He always places us where we are to learn something, change something or to be changed. Instead of making ourselves and those around us miserable and frustrating the plan of God, (which only discourages others and creates unhappiness in our surroundings), we need to seek God for His plan and purpose in the situation.

always for a divine purpose. He may place us in a job that we may not like. In situations like this we tend to show our discontent by fretting or refusing to put forth our best. However, we must be mindful that as vessels in preparation for Kingdom use, He always places us where we are to learn something, change something or to be changed. Instead of making ourselves and those around us miserable and frustrating the plan of God, (which only discourages others and creates unhappiness in our surroundings), we need to seek God for His plan and purpose in the situation.

We cannot discover God's plan while fretting. This is not part of the attributes of His workmanship, but if we can change the fret to praise, worship and thanksgiving, we would be in a much better position to hear God's instructions. The atmosphere would change, and there might even be a smile in heaven.

Children of God need to use the authority we have to change the atmosphere around us. God created us with a right spirit, governed by His Holy Spirit who is our helper to encourage us to keep ourselves in His presence always. The devil's plan for us is to keep us focused on physical things, while God's plan is for us to be sensitive to the spiritual aspect of all that is around us, so that we could be of use to God and to others.

When we are in situations that do not appease us, it is difficult to keep our focus on the things that are pleasing to God, without the Holy Spirit guiding us.

Praise and worship is of great help. In my own life as I walked in obedience to God, praise, worship mixed with prayer and fasting have helped me move from many a place in which I was stuck. During those times in His love, the Lord would always come to my rescue when I cried out. In situations like these, worship took me from one level to another, and I was able to see God taking control as gears were shifted according to His plan.

All things work for good. God was taking me out from where I was to where He wanted me to be. God's plan is perfect; that I know and His Word is sure. When He gives us a Word, we must hold on to it and do what we are called to do, no matter what we see. Stand on that word, because His Word never returns void.

We have a hope and a sure Word in Jesus Christ, and we can speak resurrection life in all trials and tribulations that come our way, if we heed the Word and allow God's light to shine through us. Remember as we go, God will, but His hands are tied when we refuse to go and do. The Holy Spirit is released to work in us when we take sides with God.

In the story of Elisha and the widow's oil, she was in need (2 Kings 4:1-7). She sought the man of God who had the answer. She needed to do two things that were very important for resolving her situation as well as to show forth God's workmanship. First she had to go and then she had to shut the door behind her, in order to focus.

Continuous work was being done in the widow. She had lost her husband and was about to lose her sons to the creditor, so she cried out to the man of God who gave her specific instructions. He checked to see what was in her possession, so he would know how to instruct her. He did the guiding, but it was her responsibility to be obedient in order to be successful.

She had a little oil, but no vessels. She was required to obtain the vessels, and together with her sons behind closed doors proceed to fill the vessels in their possession. Because they remained focused and united, all the vessels they had were filled.

This is an important lesson as to how the Potter fashions His master piece. Sometimes we do not like to go and we are reluctant to shut the door as needed. The widow's success was dependent on her focus and working in unity with her sons. They all had a common purpose. Their goal was to keep the family together safely. The sons did not question the authority of their mother, or the directions from the man of God, they just walked in obedience. They had great success as a result.

As God prepares us, He places us in specific assemblies, and as saints we are to practice to love one another as God loves us, and to be loved ourselves. Assemblies are specially geared to help us to keep focused on a common purpose as designated by God.

One of the insights I had about the process of God's workmanship and the importance of the assembly of the saints occurred while looking at an assembly line of Ford cars, as they were putting them together. When you look at a car on the road you do not know what it really takes to produce the product we see and drive.

There are all kinds of people with different abilities working in the assembly line, they function in the positions they are trained for, or for which they are best suited. In the line each person has to take responsibility for his portion, then it is passed on to the other person who adds to what was already done, and so it progresses to completion.

One of the amazing things to me was how these parts are fitted together. Sometimes they are pressed together with great force, or it may be that a small part, if left out through carelessness, could cause lots of problems. People's lives may be endangered, or they may even have to recall the particular product.

Assembling of the saints is just what it says and means. This is where we are fitted together for the Glory of God's Kingdom. There are many benefits while we are being fitted together.

Efficiency for the Body of Christ is dependent on our assembling together. We can make things easy on ourselves as individuals if we submit to God as He grooms us to be fitted together. We are groomed and fashioned according to our individual designs and purpose. The assembly is where we are perfected, as we rub shoulders with different people from all walks of life who have divine agendas. While this is so, these same people, our brothers and sisters, may have their own imperfect human agendas and wrong attitudes which they do not want to lay aside for the greater good. We therefore grind on each other while we are being chiseled by our Master Craftsman. It could be difficult and we may need to cry out at times, but let us cry out to God who will help us to see ourselves as a small part of a big performance. All of us are very important to accomplish God's plan.

In the assembly line the parts cannot feel, so it is easy for them to get the job done without resistance.

As the Potter works his clay (the saints) the process can be humiliating, discomforting even ridiculous, but necessary.

In an assembly we are called to be in the same place for the same purpose in Jesus' name and with Him as the center.

> ...loving God and our neighbour becomes easier when we are inclined to destroy the flesh in submission to God.

Love is the hallmark or trade mark of the assembly. We cannot be truly successful without loving God with all our heart, soul, mind and strength and our neighbours as ourselves. Even with this we are challenged at times, but loving God and our neighbour becomes easier when we are inclined to destroy the flesh in submission to God.

Be mindful to encourage those who need help. King Hezekiah was in some distress when he heard that the King of Assyria was coming to attack his nation Judah. He went into the house of the Lord to pray, and he encouraged those who were under him to do the same, but he started losing heart so he sent to the prophet Isaiah saying "This day is a day of trouble, and rebuke, and blasphemy; for the children have come to birth, but there is no strength to bring them forth. .. Therefore lift up your prayer for the remnant that is left."

Prophet Isaiah's positive response to the King helped him to keep his focus and reminded him of who His God was.

I am reminded of a situation when my niece was pregnant, almost due to deliver. I was at home and was led to go to her home which I did. I had no knowledge of what was happening. As I got there and inquired I was told she had gone to the hospital, but they had had no word from her or the hospital. I went to the hospital information desk, but there was no record of her delivering, so I decided I would ask permission from the desk to check the labour ward. The first hurdle was getting past the desk, but I was concerned about the length of time she was in labour. I got permission, but there was no guarantee that I would get permission upstairs.

I was taking a chance in going to the ward, because the rule is that visitors are not allowed on the ward, and as a former nurse, I knew the rules. Sometimes if there is a sister or a senior nurse in charge they may allow you to visit your patient for a moment. I got to the ward and enquired. To my surprise, without someone there that knew me, the nurse said to me "Come, she is in this room".

As I approached the bed she looked up at me and said "I cannot do it, I have no more strength". However, I could not and did not sympathise with her, but my response was, "Come on and let us praise". As I started praising she followed suit. Her mind was taken off the situation, pain and weakness seemed to lose its grip as she focused on God. I believe in about fifteen minutes or so the baby was ready to face the world, and a beautiful baby girl was born. The Holy Spirit knew the need and He quickened me to go as He obviously made the way ensuring my entry into the ward cloaking me with His favour. His workmanship was in progress even then when we were not aware. As we recognize God's continual work in us, our faith is built.

As part of His workmanship, God would often send us messages in preparation for our next assignment. The book "Prayer of Jabez" was given to me years ago by a dear friend. After reading it I started praying the prayer concerning the expansion of one's territory contained within it with no particular area of my life in mind. God however, knew where He was preparing to take me and allowed me to pray Jabez's prayer for a season. I stopped thinking about the prayer and its possible outcome, never for a moment imagining the nature or magnitude of the call that was to be given me. Sometime after this, is when the divine call came for this book to be written. Subsequently, the call was confirmed while I was reading another book in which mention was made of Jabez.

> Submitting to God's workmanship in our lives, however, requires only total obedience to His call and absolute trust in His ability to see you through it.

God does things in major ways and is able to do exceedingly, abundantly more than we could ask or think according to (His) power that works in us (Ephesians 3:20). I must emphasize dear reader, that never in a million years did this 'simple man' think of herself as an author. The degree of fear that threatened to immobilize me at the very thought of following through on this task is evidence of my absolute distrust in my ability to complete this assignment. Submitting to God's workmanship in our lives, however, requires only total obedience to His call and absolute trust in His ability to see you through it.

God's workmanship in us goes on even when we are not aware of what is happening. God puts people into our lives to chisel us under His supervision in His course of workmanship.

The quality of our experience of God's work in us depends on our response to God's sovereignty over our lives. It is God who made us and not we ourselves. We either submit, trusting Him to guide us faithfully through the assignments, or we could kick and fight, tiring ourselves out, maybe even allowing sickness to come upon us as we resist His will, like I did at one point.

As we submit to His work, like Noah our brother, we may experience embarrassment, ridicule, being laughed at etc. But the joy in the end will be ours, and the glory the Lord's.

Thank God Noah was not alone while he was going through his ordeal; he had his family. Our beloved Father has also given us a family in the Body of Christ to love, cherish and support in prayer as we work through our divine assignments. When we forsake the assembling of the saints we are neglecting the provisions that God gave to us to help us through this journey, which requires right motives and attitudes.

When I prayed Jabez' prayer, God knew what the answer would be. I never expected this impossible mission as I saw it then, because I was thinking of my ability, and not God's sovereignty.

I loved the show "Mission Impossible", but I certainly did not like this mission in the beginning. I learned when I humbled myself in the presence of God that it really was not about Jannetta at all. I am just that vessel to be used for God's Glory, and He was fashioning me for this from my early years. God's workmanship has no flaws.

Whenever I would ask God how to go about writing this book, I would hear these same words, "Study My word, and stay in My presence". On the twenty third of April 2008, God said, "Study My word- I can give you a chapter a day. I am the one doing it not you. Obey My words and I will do it. Forsake all. I need you to complete My book, it is not your book. I need it for My people, to encourage and to lift them up. It is now becoming urgent, I need a message out, My daughter."

I was still not fulfilling the plan as I should. I wrote this on a piece of paper and put it aside, not realizing the time was so far gone. I would always be distracted and did not seem to find enough time so I slacked into disobedience. I had to go before the Lord, repent to My Father, Lord Jesus and the Holy Spirit before I got back on track. I struggled a lot with the call to write this book.

It is very clear that we are God's workmanship. We were created by Him, and redeemed by Jesus Christ to show forth ALMIGHTY GOD'S GLORY through His workmanship. If I can, you can do whatever God is calling you to do. Remember it is not about you, but about Jesus- Almighty God.

Ezekiel 36 records God lifting His hands and blessing Israel, His chosen ones. They had disobeyed Him and were punished, but they were still His chosen ones. He blesses them mightily, and in verses 25-27 records, "Then I will sprinkle clean water on you, and you shall be clean; I will cleanse you from all your filthiness and from your idols. I will give you a new heart and put a new spirit within you; I will take the heart of stone out of your flesh and give you a heart of flesh. I will put My Spirit within you and cause you to walk in My statutes, and you will keep My judgments and do them." This is what you call a total make over by the Master Potter. What a GOD to behold, His mighty works to declare!

Almighty Father in the precious name of Jesus Christ, thank You for giving us the opportunity to show forth Your workmanship. You are so beautiful, we appreciate all that You are doing in our lives. Help us Lord to be receptive and to rest in Your love. We pray this in Jesus' name. Amen.

CHAPTER ELEVEN

[Tried and Tested]

Why would one need to be tested? What are the benefits of being tried and tested? Is it that there is something to be proved in testing?

Authenticity is the watch word in being tried and tested. Trials and tests are to prove who we are, where we are, and what we are made of. It shows up our strengths and or weaknesses, we are then aware of exactly what our position is. This is a true reflection of where we are. Are we exhibiting truth in the innermost parts? How do we react in a time of trouble or confrontation? What flows out of us at times like these, do we show forth Jesus and His love?

> Authenticity is the watch word in being tried and tested. Trials and tests are to prove who we are, where we are, and what we are made of.

Truth is the expression of authenticity.

An original is an original and there is really no substitute that can fulfill that place.

The manufacturer would be out of his mind or way off course, if he submits his product to a test that he knows it cannot stand up to.

Coins, gold and lots of other materials are tested for purposes of authenticity to determine, whether they are genuine or not. Many people purchase what they thought to be gold, and when tested, they recognized that they were caught off guard, because it certainly was not gold. We must remember " ALL THAT GLITTERS AND LOOKS LIKE GOLD MAY NOT BE GOLD."

Likewise, trials are all part of life and we must be open to trials and tests, allowing them to do what they are meant to do; mould, groom and fashion us for a better life. In order for us to benefit, we must be in agreement and cooperate with the Holy Spirit who is at work in our lives to see us through these times, by doing the necessary work in us.

> ...trials are all part of life and we must be open to trials and tests, allowing them to do what they are meant to do; mould, groom and fashion us for a better life.

What is that better life that we will want to be prepared for? Just as we test gold to determine if it is genuine, believers will be brought to a place where we will have to prove our true identity. Walking in Truth results in showing forth the fruit of God's Holy Spirit vs. walking in untruth which shows forth the fruit of the flesh. The fruit of the Spirit is love, joy, peace, longsuffering, kindness, goodness, faithfulness, gentleness and self-control. Whereas the works/fruit of the flesh include the total opposite e.g. adultery... uncleanness...hatred...variance...envyings...murders...revellings...(Galatians 5:19-22) ----

I have recognized, and it is so evident to me now, that over the years without these challenges, my walk may have been very different. I would not have been where I am now if the tests and trials were exempt, since trials helped me to mature and come face to face with the reality of the difference between walking in the spirit and walking in the flesh.

In a normal every day situation it is easy to appear truthful, smile and act the part of a believer. How good are we though when pressure comes to bear on us, and we feel challenged, especially when our rights are in jeopardy? Can we turn the other cheek, as we are required to do? (Matthew 5:39). Are we able to love the unlovely, to see others from the eyes of Jesus our Lord and Saviour?

What amazes me though is that when I was weak in the Lord, everything seemed huge, difficult, and so what happened in that time, was that I looked to mankind for help when it was the same mankind who was the cause of my distress. How can one really look to the cause for relief, does that make sense? No!!! Someone in sin cannot help me to come out of sin. Everything began making sense when I started seeking the Lord first. Now mind you I said, "Seeking the Lord first". There is a big difference in going to church and seeking first the Kingdom of God and His righteousness.

My mother took me to church from a baby, and I enjoyed going to church and Sunday school very much.

At a very tender age, I believe between eight and nine years I gave my life to the Lord Jesus Christ. Going to church was important, but relationship was never emphasized, and so even though I knew that I loved my Lord, I was lacking tremendously. I did well, but when the world started to pull, I was weak and I struggled, and fell many times. I thank God especially for His Grace and Mercy, and the fact that Jesus said, "On this rock I will build My church, and the gates of Hades shall not prevail against it."(Matt. 16: 18)
 I would not have been an overcomer without God's help. This is my testimony.

Thank God Jesus overcame for us, and is still interceding for us. God's perfect plan is for us to be part of His body, where our sisters and brothers support us in times of trials and tests. It is necessary that we are our brother's keeper. We need to be accountable to someone, and in this crucial time to have a prayer partner who will be a support in time of need, or even before the need arises.

Our God is a just and fair God, so He will never allow testing in areas for which He knows we are not prepared to face or in which He knows we could be destroyed. Given this fact, should we fail the test, it would not be God's fault but ours; we were most probably negligent regarding some aspect of walking in the Spirit – God's provision for overcoming trials.

How do we decide what we can trust our children with!! If your child cannot handle the responsibility of $100 would you give him or her, your bank card? Would you really?

No matter how much I love my child, I will not trust my child if he/she does not show that he/she can act responsibility. Testing is necessary, because trials are real. We will be tried in our homes and in all other areas of life, sometimes we are put in a certain place to be able to produce. With this comes a special cost. The Godly fruit of testing is invaluable to the King and His Kingdom. With this comes much pressure most times, so when the heat is turned on, our first thought is to 'get out of here, I cannot deal with this stuff.' What is amazing in this time is that other believers encourage us to do just that. If we seek God's face and inquire of Him, what should be done, the result would be entirely different, if we are obedient to His advice.

As we respond to situations, if our reactions please God He moves us up to another level, where there will be other trials and tests. Fortunately for us we have the Holy Spirit as our helper and He is there to see us through. He will quicken, guide, teach, encourage and lead us as required, if we lean on Him. He is always excited and awaiting as we ask for His help. We must be open to Him, even when He needs to correct us, and our burden will certainly be lighter.

What happens when we move away, in acts of self preservation, from those trials before the results that God is looking for in us are forthcoming, is that we hinder ourselves and need to "reset". We are now in a position where we are in a different place facing a similar or worse situation, starting all over again like the rebellious Israelites, who during their exodus from Egypt, were forced to go round the mountain for many years as opposed to days because their response to God was not what He desired. Be sensitive to the Holy Spirit and let Him be in charge of your walk in this time, and you will be victorious in all that you do.

Jesus said to cast our burdens upon Him, but we take them upon ourselves and when we meet the obstacles we turn off, leaving ourselves open for the enemy to overpower us, when we have the power to be more than a conqueror.

Remember, "The devil is like a roaring lion seeking whom he may devour" I Peter 5:8

Praise God! We have the victory if we walk in God's Will.

During the process of testing, it is only when we decide to stand firmly on God's promises and His Word that we clearly see how the enemy, who is happy to devour us, was trying to take us take us off God's track. The tests and trials become so much easier than before, maybe because we see the writing on the wall, and know, we cannot give way to the enemy. This is why God always told His children, "Be strong and be of good courage for I am with you always." Testimony — I can think of quite a few instances in my own life and even with others when this was surely a matter of concern.

A certain young lady was part of a group where she ministered for the Lord, it became very challenging for her. She felt that the head of the group did not favour her, so she felt she could not endure it any longer and was prepared to leave. For her everything was horrible, she *knew* God did not want her there any longer. She herself is telling me all of this, convinced that she is right.

I listened, asking the Holy Spirit to be my hearing and understanding. As she spoke, I felt strongly that this response would set her back in her walk with the Lord, so she needed to stay focused on Him and not on the situation. We discussed what was happening, and I expressed to her my feelings and did not think she should give up. She considered it and went before God seeking His face. She decided to stay and wait on the Lord. As she turned her focus away from the situation and on the Lord, one day she recognized all was well.

Not too long afterwards, she came to me reporting that as she stood on the Word of God, breakthrough came, and she recognized that it was a test. Thank God she passed the test. Excitement and Joy were all over her to let the world know how happy she was that God came through for her, yet another time. With this experience it allowed her to see clearly that the enemy came to steal, kill and destroy what she was called to do by Almighty God. This helped to build her faith, and God was able to take her to another level.

Some time ago there was a major tragedy in a church in Charleston, South Carolina. This incident was all over the World News, very distressing---Nine people shot to death, in a Bible study in a "CHURCH". The Pastor in charge, another Pastor and seven members of that church are studying the Word of God, their relatives are not expecting bad news, they were looking for their return home, but they did not return.

What would be the state of your mind, your heart should you get the news that a lone gun man comes into Bible study and sits in the Bible study, then the news comes that they were shot by him. I am sure you will agree that this is a major test, trial, challenge, call it what you may. It could not have been easy. I know because I personally experienced an encounter with violence through which I lost my son.

Relatives, family members were hurt, angry, and emotional. How were they to react? The day after this ordeal, less than twenty four hours after, the first hearing takes place and the Judge asks the victims' family members if they have any comments to make.

I sat in awe, as I heard the comments of close relatives. The words spoken were definitely reflections of our Master and Lord Jesus Christ. Words of love, letting the accused know that they forgive him, they are hurt, but he is forgiven. Telling him to go to God and ask God to forgive him. Not one word of hate was spoken, they truly passe that test, in their time of pain and distress. I believe the enemy was furious, these words of love captivated the entire area, and instead of fury and division, unity and peace and love have taken over. What a Joy to see the people of God rise up to be counted as Sons of God. This is a mighty testimony for the world to see, love exhibited when the presence of God is in control. I pray that children of God will take and use this as a true example of how God would want us to respond in times of adversity, when we are tried and tested. Praise be to God, this is a difficult one, and it can only be the Spirit of God and His mighty presence at work here to accomplish this task in us.
People of God, brothers and sisters be soaked in the mighty presence of God and His Word always. This is the only way.

Prayer----Almighty God and Everlasting Father I thank You for Your love and Your presence with us always. Thank You Holy Spirit for quickening us to be obedient to the Word of God, by helping us to overcome challenges and recognizing when we are to stand still and see the salvation of our God. Help us Lord because it is only with Your help that we can achieve victory, in Jesus Christ name. Amen

CHAPTER TWELVE

[Learning Through Experiences]

On leaving my home one day to attend a number of meetings at my home church, I observed a man in his late sixties sitting on the curb a few houses away. Seeing him I wondered about his situation, but I left because he seemed to be in no apparent danger, nevertheless it was a strange sight.

I went on my way, and on returning home later in the evening as it was getting dark, the situation awaited me. As I walked home on the street where I lived one of my neighbours, a young man, met me and told me about this guy who was sitting on the curb opposite my house. Approaching my home, neighbours from about four or five households were outside talking. I recognized the guy to be the same one who was sitting on the curb earlier that day. His head was bent low, long hair falling over his face and shoulders, a man of light complexion, appearing to be Caucasian.

I approached the neighbours and enquired about what was happening. The report was that this man was sitting on the curb for quite a number of hours. He was not talking or responding to anyone. He was just there with his head bent low as I had seen him earlier. Thinking that he was ill, they tried to get him to the hospital by ambulance, but the ambulance did not carry him. I had no answers. I heard all that was said, and I wondered what could be done.

I left and went into my home. My three daughters were all excited giving me the story about this man, and judging from their expressions, they were looking at me for answers. I was quiet. I had no answers, but I could see in their facial expressions the question, "Mummy, you must know what to do."

A little later on, as they were preparing for bed, I called them and we all came together in my room to pray for the man. They were all for it and we prayed. When the prayer ended, I felt the Holy Spirit saying, "Now go out to him". I passed on to them what I was guided to do and anxiously they said, "Mummy, go outside to him to do what?!" I could not answer. I did not know, but I was ready to go. So they changed their clothes and we stepped out of the gate.

Earlier while we had been praying, a group of people came from a prayer meeting and I could hear them from my room speaking to him. He did not reply, and would not even move his head. There was no response whatsoever from him. As we got outside, they were leaving. I spoke with them to see if I missed anything that I could work with, but nothing seemed to be different.

As I walked on, my girls stood close by him, but, while I was talking to my neighbours, I noticed that my girls were bending down talking to him. Then after awhile, I heard a voice that was not theirs, and as I turned I saw that he had raised his head and was chatting with the girls. The youngest one took a woogie out of her hair and was pulling his hair back to place it in the woogie. We were all amazed. I went over to them and they could tell me so much, who he was, where he lived and even the name of a friend of his. The reason she was pulling back the hair into the woogie was in response to his request to cut his hair off because it was bothering him. She convinced him to put it up and out of the way.

In confirmation to what they were telling me, I spoke with him and received the same information that he had given to them. While talking with him, it dawned on me that he had been sitting there for at least seven hours and was in need of something to eat or drink. I left them and went up quickly, blended a fig punch, poured out a little to see if he would drink it, and yes he did, all of it. I then gave him the remainder of it. Now I could not leave him on the road, so I spoke to them and we helped him up. With great effort, we managed to get him up our stairs, and on my porch. I decided to get the crib mattresses and sheets, and as we were about to make up a bed for him, he jumped up as vibrant as ever and said "I must go now! I need to take care of some business". He explained that he would return but that he must go immediately.

The man that we had helped to get up the stairs, now skipped down the stairs and was at the gate. One of the girls, the youngest, was pleading with me not to let him go. "Where is he going? Mummy! Mummy! You cannot let him go!" But with the speed at which he moved I knew that there was nothing I could do. I was taken aback by the whole turn around. It took me awhile to get to the landing and by that time he bade us goodbye, reassuring us that he would return. In no time he was at the corner.

I explained to the children that I could not hold him at my home. He had rights and was seemingly okay. It was mind boggling though. What was the message here?

I still had no explanations. What I learned the following day caused me to 'stand in my shoes and wonder'. He was around our street, but higher up from the night before. The police were called, the ambulance had taken him to the hospital but the very next morning he was back on the street and he worked his way up to our area.

Why? Who was this man? I looked for him on the streets for weeks. One day I thought I saw him – a real look-alike – but on enquiring, this man had a different name. What I know is, this man was here and he left. Did we entertain an angel? I do not know.

Let brotherly love continue. Do not forget to entertain strangers for by so doing some have unwittingly entertained angels Hebrews 13:1,2) From my experience I know that God uses these things to teach us, to train us and I am sure the young minds will never forget this experience. It was a learning experience for us.

Have your thoughts been stimulated? How would you have reacted?

God I pray that You will guide us by Your Holy Spirit to learn all that is necessary for us in our walk at this time. May we fulfill Your perfect will in our lives, so that Your kingdom come and Your will be done on earth as it is in heaven. Lord I ask this in Jesus Christ precious Name. Amen.

CHAPTER THIRTEEN

A Battle Won vs. Winning a Battle

Battles! Battles! Is this about fighting? Oh! Yes definitely. Have you ever fought? Did I ever fight? Yes, I have fought many battles, and I continue to fight at sixty plus years of age. One of my greatest battles has been scripting this book. If we were not faced with battles, something would be drastically wrong, and the scriptures would not have recorded 2 Chronicles 20: 15 "Do not be afraid nor dismayed because of this great multitude, for the battle is not yours, but God's." This tells us that God expects us to have battles, but we must hand them over to Him, responding to them only as He directs. So therefore, the question is not whether or not we will have battles, but how we fight them, and how many are won.

As a child, having older siblings was a great advantage to me in many ways. Communicating with adults became easier, and I was able to be very comfortable in the presence of my peers as well as in that of adults. This ability equipped me to be able to assist those around me in whatever way I could regardless of their age or walk in life. My teachers took advantage of this quality, and I stayed connected to them, even after leaving school.

It is my belief, and became my experience, that the youngest child in a family, tends to show a stronger sense of security, as well as a maturity beyond that of his peers. As I interacted with friends, this enhanced my ability to respond to situations in a different way, which prepared me for major battles ahead.

Moreover, I was still fairly reserved or quiet, and somewhat of a loner. I never really felt the need to identify with any group, so I laughed and talked to all with whom I came in contact. Never seeing myself as one who engaged in conflict or confrontation, I would go about my business not waiting on anyone. I didn't realize that some of my peers had a problem with my disposition. Time would reveal that this attitude would result in under currents and after effects.

Given my mother's experience with my older siblings, she established an excellent rapport with all the teachers. This resulted in her having always being kept abreast of all the school's activity. It proved to be both an advantage and disadvantage, but certainly helped me to display the behaviour that was expected of me, while preparing me for my future.

While attending elementary school, I was everybody's friend or so I thought. There were a few of us who lived in the same area and who would normally walk home together. As soon as school ended, those who were ready to leave walked together, if others lingered for too long; I made my way out of the school, with the group, and was homeward bound.

I remember this girl, who lived a few blocks from my home. She would hit one or more of us and run down the hill laughing as she approached her home. I did not like her behavior and I told her so, yet she continued. Everyone else would chase her but to no avail, because she had a head start. Recognizing this, she would erupt into laughter making a dash into her yard. I did not venture there. On the one hand, I did not intend to fall on the hill, and on the other, I was on the chubby side and not the greatest runner. As I reflect now with greater knowledge, I believe this was just her way of identifying, while saying goodbye to us.

It turns out that it was a blessing for me that I had told my mother what was happening and had asked her to talk with the girl's mum, something which she did not get around to doing.

One afternoon, while walking home, I happened to have my ruler in my hand. Normally it would be in my school bag. As usual, this dear child struck out at me and ran. By reflex action, I threw the ruler which went soaring into the air. As was her custom she turned around to laugh at us, but unfortunately the ruler was heading straight towards her and I saw terror in her face as she raised her hands to shield her face. I remained in shock as blood dropped from her hands and onto her uniform. She continued running, and as she turned a second time, I saw great fear etched on her sweet little face.

I thought to myself, what have I done? Needless to say I was very concerned, and also somewhat afraid. I had no idea at that time where she was struck. While I could not speak, the others laughed because they felt she deserved it. We were all irritated by her behavior but this was not the end that I wanted. To them I looked like a champion, scoring points with my straight throw, but personally I was sad. Fighting, as an end result, was never my style, I sometimes engaged in 'play-fighting', and did not even like it, but to know that I had hurt someone, to the extent of shedding blood was a painful blow.

I acted without thinking! Of course her mother came to my home, and my mum dealt with the situation with the understanding and love of God. Because she knew the history behind it, I was not punished. I am truly sorry for that incident! This is one of the things in my life that I wished had never occurred. Among my many regrets, this remains one.

Many years later, having lived abroad for years and now married with three children, I returned to my home in Trinidad and Tobago. On my way to a certain home to make some inquiries, a lady came out, and invited me in and greeted me with a smile. She looked familiar, I was not sure who she was, but I needed to get information from someone in this home. On entering the house, I greeted her and her mother and she then said to her mum, "Do you remember the person who gave me my life mark?" Awestruck! I saw a scar over her eye, and thought I was seeing through a magnifying glass, it looked so huge. (Mind you, she said it all laughingly but I certainly could not laugh, since I felt like the earth could open up and swallow me whole). I apologized profusely to both she and her mum. She said that it was okay, but I was embarrassed to see such a prominent scar.

There have been a few other defensive actions along my path, and even though no missiles were involved, I supposedly won, but never felt victorious. Then why fight? Why do battle?

Just before Jesus died on the cross, He said, "It is finished." This statement put quite a number of things to rest permanently. With His death, beatings, scars, stripes, abuse and shame ended our physical battles.
Ephesians 6:12 records, "For we wrestle not against flesh and blood, but against principalities and powers, against the rulers of the darkness of this age, against spiritual hosts of wickedness in the heavenly places." NKJV.

Do I still fight? Of course! I am still challenged, but now I fight victorious, joyful battles. I refuse to defend myself physically anymore and if I am about to get caught up in a physical battle, I will be quickened in my spirit to stop. In so doing, if I am obedient I can stay clear of all that will not glorify my God. The Spirit of God is so very helpful to keep our behavior on track when we desire to exalt His Name as we respond through His Word. The Holy Spirit reminds us of the scripture, "For the battle is not ours but God's." What greater joy than to know that we are at liberty to fight battles marshalled by God himself, knowing that He surrounds us and is always on our side. We will always win the battle when we allow Him to be our defender. Also recognizing that the devil is the true enemy, and that he is not worthy of my apology, nor should he cause me to have regrets , gives me more determination to stand on God's Word.

Having learned over the years that life is about battles on every level, I give praise and thanks to God for the ministry in which He has placed me for training in His army. If we are in an army, then we must know that there will be battles. With some battles you may not see the results, but by faith you know that the battle is already won. As children of God we have the victory, Hallelujah!

Normally, when a battle is won there is a victory shout. If there is no victory shout, one is led to believe that the battle is lost, but this is not literally so. Even when I do not see physical results, there is such a sweet presence of God that signals a great victory shout deep inside of me.

The evidence is, knowing in my spirit that the devil has many blood scars, for all the battles that believers have fought on their knees. The Jesus I serve is "The Victor" always. This makes me excited and more eager to battle, giving me fervor to encourage others to fight and not give up, while envisioning victory. By faith I am sure my children and blood line are already in the Kingdom of GOD. By faith I have no more concern about them once I stay in obedience to my Lord. By faith I can see them seated in heavenly places with the Lord Jesus Christ.

When I think of a battle I see David as a mere boy. When David recognized that the Philistines, especially the giant Goliath, was belittling the army of the living God, he was very upset. He could not stand by and allow this to happen, certainly not to His beloved God's army. As a shepherd boy having had such serious experiences resulting in victory, he felt he had to make use of them. David recognized and gave glory and honour to God for keeping him safe and seeing him through every situation. Victory over a lion and tiger without obvious weapons is no small task. I can imagine David feeling such confidence as he remembered that with God at the helm, all his battles had been won.

Reflecting on the power of an awesome God, he concluded that no battle can be compared with His great power. He knew he had won big battles as a shepherd boy, and he definitely knew in whose name they were won.

With this revelation, David was able to agree with 1 Samuel 17:26, "For who is this uncircumcised Philistine, that he should defy the armies of the living God?" "I am coming to get you" would probably be my answer if I were in David's shoe.

Not for one moment, must it be taken for granted that this readiness just happens. As I reflect on David and think of my years of preparation, I can clearly see that from birth my armour was being fitted. God places us in specific families, communities, schools and environments which play an integral part in developing our personalities while preparing us for the future assignments He earmarked for us. The family within which God places us, contributes to our uniqueness, training, disciplines, experiences, abuse, loving care, blessings or curses. They are all eventually used for His Kingdom's purpose. We may not always see this, because the situations are so devastating, perhaps even cruel.

Doubtless David as the youngest, with older siblings who may have pushed him around, was developing strength as part of his training for where God was taking him. He would not have been aware that his armour was being fitted bit by bit for God's purpose and destiny. David's armour, its size and shape were designed for his anointing to serve in the capacity in which God had called him. The armour is custom designed for each person and purpose.

David stepped forth to stand up in love for the army of the living God against the Philistine giant Goliath, not recognizing that he was really the giant in God. While King Saul agreed to his going out, and tried to outfit him with his physical armour, David was not aware that he was already in full battle gear because he was armed spiritually. In his physical armour David was uncomfortable, but he was about to fight a battle which required spiritual armour. Battles can be destructive if fought in the physical. So David, knowing his God, and with the surety that the battle was already won, threw off the armour and went forth with his God fitted armour and his last words to the giant. 1 Samuel 17: 47 "Then all this assembly shall know that the Lord does not save with sword and spear; for the battle is the Lord's, and He will give you into our hands." God had already begun to equip David for his journey in life as a man after God's own heart, so he charged towards the giant seeing clear victory.

> David stepped forth to stand up in love for the army of the living God against the Philistine giant Goliath, not recognizing that he was really the giant in God.

David had a sweet relationship with his God, to the point that he understood that he was created in His image and likeness, reflecting a similar position in the battle. In his position of surrender to God, he demonstrated to us a fine example, of who we can be in Christ as victorious people. Utilizing David as our example, we too will be better conditioned to have our customized armour designed as He wills.

As believers if we try to wear someone else's armour, we run the risk of being wrongly outfitted, walking where we are not called, fighting other people's battles, and trying to be who we are not called to be.

As I mature in Christ, I can bless God as I understand how God's grace and mercy reached out to me. Furthermore, I am more appreciative of how my experiences groomed me to be the person that I am today, and continuing to help me become a victorious woman in battle, in Christ Jesus! By no means is it an easy road, but I am able to empathize with persons in diverse situations, which is all part of God's plan.

This scripture should mean a lot to us, Romans 8: 28 "And we know that all things work together for good to those who love God, to those who are the called according to His purpose." NKJV. If we love the Lord, and are called by His purpose then nothing is really meant to harm us.

With this in mind, it is very clear that jealousy, envy, and malice, is out of place in our lives. These emotions cause trouble, and open doors for the devil to enter and disrupt God's work. We need to be aware of our heart condition in all that we do, determining how we respond to God's love, which would help us to stand in the evil day. What is the armour which assures us of security and protection in battle?

As a soldier wears physical armour, so does the child of God wear spiritual armour. This armour is fitted, but is activated as we come into alignment with God's plan for our lives and as we believe and accept His salvation plan, with His son Jesus Christ as Lord of our life. As we receive this Truth, by hearing the Word of God, our loins are girded with truth, strengthening us, and keeping us in good spiritual shape to fight the good fight of faith.

The helmet of salvation is placed on our head, so we are protected from head on collisions as we go forward with the Word of God. As we understand that we are now the righteousness of God in Christ Jesus, by faith we are offered Righteousness.

Righteousness now becomes our breastplate, which is ours through Jesus the only Righteous one. Moving on we are adorned with our sword and shield.

The right hand exhibits the Sword of the Spirit which is the Word of God, to be used against the devil as he comes, and in the offensive to prepare us to resist the enemy. It cuts asunder all evil because it is sharper than any two edged sword.

The Shield of Faith is obviously in our left hand, signifying that we are able to block the fiery darts as they come, especially as we allow the Word to rise within us and take control.

Our feet are made for walking, carrying the good news of the Gospel, and are shod with the preparation of the Gospel of peace. In Christ Jesus we experience the peace of God and are to pursue it with our fellow men. This for me is like "icing on the cake," As we walk in peace regardless of our circumstances, and live in peace with others, in spite of offences, we clearly demonstrate that Jesus the Prince of Peace, Lives within us. People may not hear us, but witnessing our trials, they are definitely moved by the Peace within us, that passes all understanding.

I pray Almighty God that as we fight our battles, we may stay connected to the source, and in Jesus' Name we pursue the fight the way You taught us to, not in our own might and strength, but with the help of the Holy Spirit. Lord of Hosts our mighty Captain, cause us to remember that any battles fought without You are lost. May our spirits receive the great commission to which You God have called us, so that we would have pretty feet running to take the gospel, highlighting Jesus the Prince of Peace. As we take Your Gospel out Lord, we will be spreading the Gospel of peace and not war, in Jesus Christ precious Name. Amen.

The complete armour is necessary in order to stay alert and on course. Otherwise, we will keep fighting battles that never make sense and people will end up scarred like my school mate; scars that cannot be erased even if we wanted them to be.

No mercy is due the devil, so let us get in line with God and His Word. As God's army, let us join forces, forging forward relentlessly, gaining ground over the devil. Then our records will reflect battles won victoriously!

CHAPTER FOURTEEN

[Visa Time]

A few years ago one of my very good friends had a death in her family. Her sister, who lived in the U.S.A., died unexpectedly and she wanted me to be there with the family. Her other sister who lives in the deep south of Trinidad, did not have a visa and needed to get one in order to attend the funeral. Realizing this, I decided I would help her by making sure she had all the documents required. Under normal conditions a visa application can be complicated, especially if you have never applied for one.

Can you imagine the turmoil she was in after receiving this shocking news and not knowing where to begin with this process? I decided that I would walk her through the process and accompany her to the U.S. Embassy.

Thankfully I had just dealt with the Embassy when a close relative of mine died, and I had all the information that was required for such a visa. This was really a blessing, and I was glad to be of assistance, especially at this time of overcoming the shock and dealing with the loss. The plan was that she would apply for the visa first and then her family would purchase her ticket.

My friend, who also lives in the U.S.A., asked me to get in touch with her sister, and let her know that I would assist her. I did contact her and she was happy to know that I was prepared to help. I live in the Port of Spain vicinity, very close to the Embassy and on a good day it could take over two hours to travel from her home to mine.

Knowing the distance, I knew it would be difficult for her travelling back and forth, so I thought it would be best for her to be prepared with all that was needed both for the visa and her trip to the U.S.A. I informed her of the documents that she needed, and suggested that she come prepared for the trip by bringing her bags with her. She had limited time in which to acquire the visa since the sister's family did not want to wait too long to make arrangements for the funeral.

She arrived later than planned and without key documents required for the visa application process. It was now Friday and we would have to get the other documents sorted and ready for the Embassy on Monday. Clearly now it was too late for her to get to the States in time for the funeral, which was scheduled for early the following week. Realizing this, I decided that I would not go to the funeral as was planned, but I would stay and assist her in applying for the visa. She would at least be able to visit with the family and be there for a memorial service planned shortly after.

We spent the time usefully; got all the documents sorted out and we discussed the circumstances surrounding this sudden death. Her sister went to work and never returned home, without any notice this fairly young mother was leaving behind a husband, a teenager and an eleven year old.

Since this seemed to be God's plan, I had to tune my ears to hear in what direction He would lead me.

With this fresh in our minds, I saw the need to emphasize the importance of being prepared for death and to meet with God no matter how young or old one might be.

She decided to spend the weekend with me instead of going all the way home. This was time well spent; she was able to air her feelings while I lent a listening ear. Being more relaxed and having things ready for the Embassy, she accompanied me to our Worship service that evening where she surrendered her life to the Lord. She was so, very happy, that she had the opportunity to make this very important decision. She grew up going to church, but moved away from where she knew she was supposed to be, so it was a joy to return. God used this opportunity to speak to her heart and she responded to His calling while the Spirit drew her back to Him. We all joined her in thanking God for His love, mercy and divine appointment.

On Monday we went to the Embassy and she was granted a visa. It was a blessing for her to be able to visit with her family and join them for the memorial service. They all looked forward to her arrival.

God always has a plan and we must be in tune with Him for His plan to be fulfilled. He had a divine appointment set up for her in the midst of this trying time of her sister's death. God's plan also initiated changing my plan to accommodate her. His plan and design is so perfect, and once we allow Him the freedom, He initiates things in order, which He did, allowing me the opportunity to partner with Him. I am glad that I was able to be directed by Him, even though at the time I cannot say I heard a voice, but inside of me I did what I felt needed to be done and I felt His peace while doing it. God knew what the outcome would have been, I did not know, but He is Almighty and All knowing and He will always have His way.

I pray that we the children of God would lay ourselves aside and let Him shine forth in us, no matter how we think or feel. He works all things out for good to them that love Him, help us Lord to remember that You are in control always and that You know the desired effect in all circumstances. We thank You Lord that we can trust You with our lives and all that concerns us. We pray this in Jesus' Name. Amen.

CHAPTER FIFTEEN

[Decision Time]

As God's purpose arose in my heart to help people see Jesus, astonishing things would unfold. To this end, there was a time of decision.

I found that my Lord would put me in places where there was a great need. Without the shadow of a doubt, I was aware that it was the working of the Holy Spirit, allowing my spiritual eyes and ears to see and hear. This always resulted in alerting me and helping me to fulfill God's purpose and destiny. Sometimes there may be a stirring within me and at other times, I felt as though I was acting out a prearranged action program. Some of these occasions have a degree of sacrifice attached. From my experience, the greater the sacrifice, and the degree of importance or urgency associated with the matter, the greater the resulting testimony.

One such occasion was during a Greyhound bus trip from Atlanta to Florida when my seventeen year old son Godfrey was on scholarship at Morehouse College in Atlanta. He could not come home to Trinidad that particular year, so I decided a surprise visit would be nice. He was very young and I knew that he missed home greatly, even though he never complained. In order to make the trip economically feasible, riding the bus was always my first choice, and I enjoyed the Greyhound bus ride. There was always someone of interest on the trip, and in my spirit, I would eagerly anticipate these God ordained encounters. A few of my trips were five to six days long, yet I loved the experience.

This night in particular, with my ticket in hand and having checked departure and arrival times to facilitate my brother picking me up in Florida, my son arranged for a friend to take us to the departure terminal in Atlanta.

We ensured that we got to the terminal early so that there would be no hitches. After checking in, we waited for the call to board the bus, but departure time was approaching and nothing seemed to be happening. I got a little anxious wondering, "Did I somehow miss the bus, what if I needed to purchase another ticket? Where would I get the funds"?

Without exhibiting my anxiety, I went to the counter and was relieved to hear that the bus was delayed. Time moved on and still there was no bus. We waited and kept checking. Four hours later, we still had no idea what was happening. It was frustrating, mainly because there was no information given. We did not know whether we would leave during the night or on the next bus. I was pretty calm but I was sorry that my son and his friend had to wait this long. While they had no intention of leaving me, until they were sure that I was on the bus and all was well, his friend was upset. He stated emphatically that he was going to put in a claim for the inconvenience and we agreed. If we were given a specific time the bus was to leave, we may have planned to leave and return, which would have been more relaxing for us all. I was not (unduly) perturbed because I truly felt God was in control, and the inconvenience must have been for a particular reason, which could result in a God story!

Finally we heard an announcement for the bus, rejoicing and relieved, we hugged and said good bye. I thanked them for keeping me company, and apologized for the hours of delay. They accompanied me to the bus, but never left until the bus was on its way. This delay certainly did not destroy the beautiful vacation I had with Godfrey.

As I sat, I realized that the bus would be full, and having given God permission to place whomever He wanted to sit next to me, I waited and wondered who it would be. Then a gentleman who appeared to be in his late thirties came and sat next to me. I greeted him and had little conversation at that time, but he did tell me his final destination. I was tired and it was just past midnight so I wanted to sleep for the first four hours to the next stop. The journey began and all seemed well. I dozed off, waking up when the driver announced that we were approaching our stop. We all had to get off the bus while it was being cleaned.

Fortunately, I learned from my experiences to sit in a position in the station where I could view the departure gate and the bus. While waiting for the announcement on the public address system for those with boarding passes to re-board the bus first, I saw the driver go to the gate and realized that he was about to resume the trip. I re-boarded and noticed that my seat mate had not returned, yet new passengers started boarding. I told those persons who came to ask if the seat was available, that someone was sitting there. Then feeling that I needed to make a decision on his behalf, I took something and put it on the seat to show that it was occupied. The driver neglected to make a departure call, so he had no idea what was happening.

He eventually decided to check, and was shocked to find that the driver had already allocated his seat to someone else. But God had me block that seat because of His divine plan. He and the driver argued, both seeing themselves as being right. The driver insisted that he must get another bus and he refused to get off the bus. He retorted that he was on this bus and no call was made to return. Through all this, I just prayed and eventually the driver gave way and he came to his seat.

God is a great God, awesome in all His ways and plans. Gracious and truly Merciful is our God. Our words, actions, and deeds certainly cannot give God all the Glory He deserves.

That gentleman came and sat down and we chatted for a short while about the situation, then we thanked God for allowing him back on the bus. He then stretched into his bag and took out an old coverless Bible, my spirit rejoiced as I saw the opening God was giving me. In this I allowed God by His Holy Spirit to lead as I recognized God had organized it all, even to seating us together, although the enemy tried hard to abort the plan.

Feeling comfortable, and somewhat relieved that I had stood up for him, he opened up and explained that he was returning to a crime scene from which he had fled. He shared that he was in a common law relationship and even though they both attended

Church and Bible Study, they had different expectations regarding their relationship and there was a lot of emotional baggage.

It was such a complicated situation. He was convinced that she did not want to marry him because her income was more than his, and they were professionally in different brackets. He did not handle the emotional strain well and ended up in conflict with the law due to incidents involving abuse against his partner. He decided to run from the police and had been on the run for a few months.

God the Father, Jesus the Son and the Holy Spirit was there and enabled me to help him see Jesus and His plan for his life. In his running, the Father started drawing him to the Saviour, Jesus the Christ, and the Holy Spirit was already doing what needed to be done. As he opened up to me, God used me to counsel him and this confirmed what God had already begun to do in his life. He thanked God and me as he made that very important decision, without hesitation, he recommitted his life to God. Both he and his girl friend had started reconciling a while before and were both starting to see things differently. They recognized that their lives were not honouring God and were now prepared to make it right. He was also ready to face the consequences of his previous actions and believed that God did not want him hiding any more. They were now ready to make the necessary changes to first honour God in their lives. I knew that God touched him and this was truly a divine appointment.

I may never see him again on this side of heaven, but if we continue to serve our Merciful and Gracious God I surely will see him in heavenly places.

This and other incidents like it prove to me how great God's love is and that whatever is for us we will always receive. It reminds me of Peter, how he loved the Lord and even though at a particular point he failed Him, Peter was still able to go on to feed Jesus' sheep. (John 21: 15-17).

On my arrival at my brother's home, I called my son and told him the God story. The testimony was so powerful that I knew I had to withdraw my agreement and cancel the claim that his friend was planning to file against the bus company for the inconvenience caused.

I am more and more amazed at God's mighty hand of deliverance and sustenance. He has all things under His control.

Father I thank You that Your hand was upon this young man and his girlfriend, also Lord that Your hand is upon us. Help us to make right decisions at the right time, for today is our day of decision. Help us to recognize Your plan in our lives as You give us the opportunity to show forth Your love, mercy and grace to others around us. We thank You for giving us opportunity after opportunity to show forth Your Glory, as You gave one of Your sons and his potential wife an even greater opportunity to experience abundant life. Thanks and praise to the Almighty God who knows all things before the foundation of the world. Thank You Father, in Jesus Christ precious Name. Amen.

CHAPTER SIXTEEN

[Train Up a Child, and Let Him Go]

While standing in my kitchen contemplating whether I should make banana punch (smoothie) for my grand children, Jamal one of the younger ones came to chat with me and on mentioning the banana smoothies, he cheered, "Yes Granny! Yes! Yes!"

I agreed and he presented his recipe, giving me directions. It included bananas, milk, honey, vanilla essence, oats, peanut butter, and then, "Granny, Granny! guavas!" Of course I stopped before adding the peanut butter because it would no longer be banana punch; it would be a mêlée.

He was little and so excited that he wanted to add whatever ingredient he desired. I am sure even he would not have been happy drinking it, if I had complied with his wishes.

Our training of children today has become a flavour that is not recognizable, just like this punch would have been. Sometimes when I hear certain things, I have flash backs to this story, so mixed up that there is no particular identity, it just stands for whatever goes.

As we train God's children for Kingdom use, we ourselves must clearly understand what God requires of us. As parents we should ask ourselves "Do I have what it takes?" Am I where God wants me?" Where will my guidance come from? What changes do I need to make before venturing into such an important area, since I will now be responsible for nurturing a soul in preparation for a lifetime?

In my own experience of training my children, I was only able to teach them what I knew. Was it fair then to expect of them something different than what they were taught?

Years ago we were taught to go to church, possibly accept the Lord and live a good life. Basically that was it. Once we attended church, there was no emphasis on how we lived the remaining six days of the week. This was acceptable for most of us, however, those who had an awareness or got a call for a deeper walk with the Lord, were considered weird if you obeyed God's call, and lived a life governed by His Word and His Holy Spirit.

> Years ago, children were taught to respect older members of the family. They were allowed or encouraged to visit the elderly in the community and share with them, and to help them if they needed assistance. Now each person just cares for themselves, so the children are taught to be selfish and even disrespectful to others in many ways. We must see the need to rectify this by repairing this breach of servant hood.

But God really wants this 'strange' or 'peculiar' walk with Him. He wants us training our children via His Word even from the womb. As they grow, these qualities would be exhibited to those around us- expressions of love, truth, righteousness, holiness, peace and worship etc. For our children to be true worshippers, our lifestyle must be that of a true worshipper. Jesus must be reflected in all areas of our lives with agape (love) as our guide. We will only be as strong as what is inside of us. This is true in the physical as well as in the spiritual. A well presented lady, may leave a much different impression when you become acquainted with her.

Jesus was the perfect teacher, who taught His disciples and those around Him how to respond, care and love. He had great compassion, yet He disciplined when necessary. His true personality was seen every day as He lived out the Father's nature. We too must exhibit to those around us a lifestyle of integrity and honour to show forth to the world God's peace and our rest in Him. We must be mindful that children are only children for a short time, and so our focus on them should be priority in their early years.

We may not all be officially engaged in teaching children. Our 'classrooms' do not have walls, so we must remember that we are always on display whether we want to be or not.

Children will copy what they see and hear, regardless of what they are told. If you tell them to say please, thank you or may I, and you do not speak to them in the same manner, they are not going to respond willingly to your request.

Much of Jesus' teachings were taught through serving others, yet servant hood is an area most of us shy away from. We want to be served not to serve. We must revisit our foundation, Jesus Christ, and the rock on which He built His Church in order for us to move forward. Many families are in crisis and this is reflected in the church and in the world.

Years ago, children were taught to respect older members of the family. They were allowed or encouraged to visit the elderly in the community and share with them, and to help them if they needed assistance. Now each person just cares for themselves, so the children are taught to be selfish and even disrespectful to others in many ways. We must see the need to rectify this by repairing this breach of servant hood.

True servant hood is only achieved when the love of God is resident in our hearts, and love becomes our guide, remembering this love is Jesus Christ. Our first step in training children is to love God and to love each other; not to speak love, but be love. It is easy to speak love, until the crunch comes and it gets tough, that is when the fruits are exhibited.

Serving is Christ and Christ is serving.

My greatest accomplishment came through serving in the Kingdom of God for the cause of Jesus Christ. Most times it is sacrificial, but lovely.

Training starts from as early as the womb. I would definitely encourage parents once they are planning children to start preparing the ground way before conception, by lifting up these children in prayer. Washing of the sperm and the egg should be done using the blood of Jesus, while declaring the Lordship of Jesus Christ over them as they are dedicated to Almighty God.

Early dedication of children to God, together with the commitment to keeping them in God's presence, and fulfilling God's requirements to training up a child in the way he should go, so when he is old enough he would not depart from it, has maximum benefits. This requires reading the Word of God with them, and teaching them to love, applying scriptures and Christianity in a practical sense to living.

If love, peace and the presence of God are continually released upon the babe, it will bear Godly fruit making great difference in their lives.

I encourage parents that as they study the scriptures to include the babies by telling them what scripture is being read. Really involve them.

It would be interesting to see the results of a long term study comparing the difference of children who have been offered up to God before conception and groomed in the word of God and those who were not.

Early teaching, before habits are formed is vital. It is more difficult to retrain children as they grow older, especially if they are already influenced by their environment.

Over the years, my eyes have been opened to realizing that babies are not babies for very long anymore. They grow and mature so quickly. They seem to be born with a mandate from God to produce, so they are on the move looking carefully at all that is around them and acting accordingly, forming opinions very early, and showing forth what they see and hear.

Some of my grandchildren were praising God before they were a year old, hands up in the air before they could talk and as they grew older, they began acting out the full worship service at home.

They are like sponges and they absorb everything.

Yes there will be formal worship, teaching and devotional times, where as they study the Word, it is related to everyday living, so the scriptures are appreciated as life. As a result of these activities, they also understand the reasons why they should not do certain things. This does not mean that later on they may choose to do what they know to be wrong, but certainly it makes it more difficult for them to continue the practice, because sooner than later they will be convicted by the Holy Spirit.

I can relate to this myself. I grew up in the church and gave my life to the Lord at an early age. I was never interested in anything except activities around the church. I was very active in the church and enjoyed my experience there. Sad to say, the people who drew me away from the things of God were active church members. I believe God had me experience this to make me more aware of what really happens so I could be of use to help someone else. I backslid, but was always convicted until I returned. I never felt comfortable, and I know that the Spirit had it that way. Situations arose and people seemed unable to give the right counsel or to help me to get back on track. Deep inside of me God worked with the desire He had in me, and finally drew me back.

I thank God for my mother and her training because if I did not have these teachings to what would I have returned?

I have had the privilege of having my own children. God blessed me with five beautiful sons. He also blessed me with additional sons and daughters. I have tried as best I could to teach. Sometimes the girls would get angry with me when others could do things that they could not, especially when tough love was exercised. The toughest times were when a child or children in the church were allowed to do something that I would not allow them to do. An example of this was other children's ability to wear certain clothes, or go to certain places. The times that I would be praised by them was when the youth leader would use them as examples of how children in the group should be dressed or when the young people in general would be encouraged to do something that I had already privately shared with them.

Children are reflections of their parents. Just as the parents should be reflections of Jesus Christ.

Sons and daughters must live by every word that proceeds from the mouth of God. The Word must be deep within our spirits to equip us to respond to life's situations. Titus 1:9 talks about holding fast the faithful Word as he has been taught that he may be able by sound doctrine, both to exhort and convict those who contradict. The Holy Spirit takes the Word in our spirits and custom fits the Word to our circumstances. We must depend on Him as we train our children, since they have different personalities, and will have diverse calls. This is very important for us to recognize.
Susanna Wesley, mother of John and Charles Wesley, spent special time with each of her children. She was aware that they needed individual help and guidance. She did not see them only as a group; they were individually all powerful men and women of God.

As we train children we must consciously be in agreement with God. This agreement, done in prayer, will greatly benefit the child's future. God's plan and purpose for that child is already established in heaven. If we take a trip down memory lane to our childhood, we may be able to see things that would have influenced us for good or bad that helped to outfit us for our Kingdom's journey. God is truly an awesome God. I look at situations in my own life and see how God designed them and turned them around to benefit His work. Many of our experiences may have occurred even before we were saved or were in line with His Word, and yes He uses it all for His Glory. His mercy and grace, His favour, man's favour and God's protection were all extended to us in abundance even when we were not aware.

Basic training should be the same for all children, but we need to seek God's face for our individual children to be guided as God would require for His planned purpose in their lives. Touch base with God seeking His face for the children to be groomed for Him. He is the master mind with all blue prints.

Apostle Paul had a beloved spiritual son called Timothy. In 2 Timothy 1: 5, Paul tells us something of Timothy's background, "When I call to remembrance the genuine faith that is in you, which dwelt first in your grandmother Lois and your mother Eunice, and I am persuaded is in you also" What a legacy! This is worth more than all the tea in China. I love with all my heart this beautiful example of the result of three generations of consistent, Godly training. We need to have many more examples like this.

> Parents are not made, but become, and so we will make errors as we go. However, we expect that as we live by the Word and change the way we operate compared to when we were not in Christ, we will be better able to demonstrate to our children the reasons why living as God wills is far superior to living without God.

We can start now, if each one of us would take it upon ourselves to make a conscious Godly deposit in the lives of each child with whom we come into contact. If we do not have a child, adopt one, physically or spiritually. There must be someone that you can target for God, asking Him for guidance regarding what you could do with and for that person. Pray for that person until you see change. They may not even know that you are praying for them, but take heart, your effort will benefit the Kingdom of God. They may never know, but what we should care about is that the Kingdom of God benefits. God can and will lead you to specific children once you have a heart's desire.

Parents are not made, but become, and so we will make errors as we go. However, we expect that as we live by the Word and change the way we operate compared to when we were not in Christ, we will be better able to demonstrate to our children the reasons why living as God wills is far superior to living without God. Truth is expected to be shown in all that we do, and this is an area of great contention between parents and children throughout history. As believers, we must be transparent at all times. Those around us should be able to see the true person. If we falter, we should apologize, repent and move on. This is a progressive walk, it will not all happen in a day, but we must see changes as we go, and teach our children even with our

> As believers, we must be transparent at all times. Those around us should be able to see the true person. If we falter, we should apologize, repent and move on. This is a progressive walk, it will not all happen in a day, but we must see changes as we go, and teach our children even with our mistakes.

mistakes.

As we draw closer to God and we understand what He requires of us, we are expected to reflect Him in everything we do; which includes taking care of the entire man, watching what we eat, wear, how we look, what we think, say and do, our actions and reactions. We are also expected to have the right attitude which would determine how we treat people.

Children of God are a holy and peculiar people. So then are we expected to have our bodies exposed? My heart is sad when I know that parents, who are believers, dress their children in a manner that only reflects the world. Where is our example then?

Since my body is the temple of God, I should be treating this temple with honour and dignity. One day I got a full revelation of what it means to be the temple of the living God. Although, I was aware before, after the revelation, I began checking myself for God's purpose even more in all that I do. It is time that we truly awaken. We cannot do what we are expected to do for God through an unworthy vessel. We have to train the children from an early age to give them a better opportunity to cultivate lives which are pleasing to God.

I have seen the benefits of training even in my own children, and I have been told "thanks" for what was received in my extended family. It has not been an easy task, but an enjoyable one to see the different responses. The ones who received without much fuss are well on their way to the fulfillment of God's will in their lives. They have been able to pass the various tests and trials because of the sound training they received which anchors them in God's way. Others who were not ready, and felt they could take a different walk, are still on that road, but they too will have a mighty testimony through the rough hard road. Praise Almighty God!
Beloved, it works. Give thanks to God for His word, His Love and His truth and pray that they will prevail.

Are you a Lois or Eunice? What is it going to be? If we start now, we can get some generations lined up. It is never too late to start. Even babes in Christ could benefit from our encouragement and testimony to stir them up for growth. Let us reflect seriously about our commitment to train up the children in the way they should go.

Jeremiah 1:5 tells us "Before I formed you in the womb I knew you; Before you were born I sanctified you; I ordained you a prophet to the nations." When Jeremiah was a youth, the Lord called him and sent him not only to Judah, but to the nations. He was a prophet of God.

Proverbs 22:6 "Train up a child in the way he should go, and when he is old he will not depart from it." Do you know when you give birth to a child what God wants to use that child to accomplish in that child for His Kingdom? If we fail to train and discipline them, we are unfair to them because they will then have to be made ready in a manner that may be more difficult for them and even for us. God's will, will be done.

In this end time season the young children will be used in a mighty way. So as we train them, let us join together with God to prepare them to go forth into the world as His children.

Dear God and Father, You created us to be like You, to be Your representatives on the earth. You gave us the responsibility to make disciples, to train up our children, Your children, to be like You. Help us dear Lord to keep our focus on You, so that we can do what You require us to do, and to be pleasing in Your sight. We cannot do it without You Holy Spirit. It is totally impossible to achieve a pleasing end in Your sight without You. We destroy all that blocks us from fulfilling this assignment, and apply the blood of the Lamb upon all the children as we put a hedge of protection around them in the precious name of Jesus the Christ. Amen.

CHAPTER SEVENTEEN

[YOUNG KINGS]

Young Kings are extremely important for Kingdom building. This I believe is God's end time plan. Creation is waiting for the sons of God – Young Kings - to arise. We are given a mandate by Almighty God- Father, Son Jesus Christ and the Holy Spirit to go forth, be fruitful and multiply. God created Adam and Eve in His image and likeness, and they were supposed to produce after their own kind, which is God's image and likeness, but as Adam and Eve corrupted themselves by sin there was a default, and all mankind inherited their sin nature.

As they sinned and fell short of the Glory of God, a struggle ensued for human beings after this. God extended His hand of love to mankind. He still made it possible for man to obey Him through the laws which He gave to Moses. It is recorded in the scriptures that there were men who walked in obedience to the law and walked uprightly. They pleased God, their heart condition was solely set on God and they believed the promise of redemption through His one and only son Jesus, before the actual arrival of Jesus. They made a choice to serve God, and while choices are always challenging, that responsibility is always ours.

We become young kings as we walk in God's way, as we were created to walk. The process begins with redemption. God made provision for us through His son Jesus Christ and the redemption story. The redemption story is the most beautiful and powerful story that there will ever be. It is awesome, that God sent His son Jesus who had no sin to be the ultimate sacrifice for us, sinful man. He came from heaven to earth, showed us the way and how to live, then suffered and died on the cross for us, shed His blood for us, then He rose on the third day that we too, can rise in Him to kingship, and have eternal life. In Jesus' coming He fulfilled the law which God gave to Moses. No longer is there need for animal sacrifice, Jesus was the ultimate sacrifice for sin and its consequences, but we are now called to be a living sacrifice for Him.

With this powerful experience we can be changed in a moment from a wretched sinner to a saint, renewed in mind and thought life. Importantly though we must decide that we desire that change, and it is ours to have at no cost besides commitment and obedience.

God ordained Jesus to be groomed on earth as the first young King fit for the Kingdom. He was prepared for purpose and destiny, showing forth God's will on the earth just as it is in heaven. This is our pattern to follow, showing that it is possible to fulfil this plan of God.

In the natural world, a King comes from a royal family, and they are groomed by all the standards of the royal guidelines. They are kept apart from commoners or anyone who is not part of that heritage. They are only exposed when they are ready or old enough to represent the Kingdom, and strong enough to resist the influence of the outside world. By that time they are well trained, and know what is expected of them. They are expected to be representatives every day, twenty four hours each day.

Likewise, God says through King Solomon in His Word which is supposed to govern us—Kingdom people, "Train up a child in the way he should go, And when he is old he will not depart from it." Proverb 22: 6. In Godly wisdom, King Solomon was saying that we are to receive these cherished possessions from God, dedicate them back to Him, (which we do at the altar), but then some of us stop there. God expects us to follow and teach His Kingdom principles, and to keep them in His ways always. Part of this grooming is through guidance, discipline and encouraging to stay on the right path, but they will be lost if there is no example. This worked for the early church, and they had great power and strength to stand up and represent the King and His Kingdom, in spirit and in truth. We are to be sanctified and set aside for Him for His use, so that our daily routine will show forth His truth. But we have separated our daily routine from our church routine, and have left God out of our day to day activities. We are no longer a Holy Ghost filled people. We have neglected what we had, and now we are weakened spiritually and are producing after our own kind—a weak people with no power to stand for Jesus and what is Godly. We crumble at the slightest attack, and do not seem to have any backbone or desire to stand for what is right, so we take the easy way out by compromising. We shy away from anything that requires some form of sacrifice because it is too difficult for us to be bothered.

As parents we pamper our children, not allowing them to be responsible for small chores or activities that will help them to grow and mature wisely. Our famous line is that they are too small; they still have time, and so before you know it they are "out of hand" and "doing their own thing;" no time now to train or guide. We need to take stock now for time is short, and we are really in need of these young minds. They have a lot to contribute to the Kingdom, but they must be trained.

God chose parents for His son Jesus; remember His son was coming to a natural world through a supernatural birth, so He had to have parents who would agree with Him, to fulfil this purpose. They had to be chosen to train this young King for his role as King of Kings and Lord of Lords. God was in total control of all things then, and is still in control now. We are required to take the same stand for God with those who God has given to us to groom for this time.

Children are a special gift from God, a gift of great value. While most gifts belong to us, this one is exceptional since we are basically stewards of the children gifted to us. God can take them back without our permission and we could never love them the way He does. As we come to terms with our role as stewards of the children, let us understand there is a great responsibility of rearing these loved ones which is not to be taken lightly.

The Bible records show that young Kings have been groomed successfully before. Take Timothy for example, his grandmother and his mother took responsibility for teaching him. So then what is our problem?

We need to increase our numbers of power- packed believers (especially the young) blood washed, Holy Ghost filled and fire baptized for such a time as this. We must change our mind-set to a Godly mind- set, with a determination to produce after God's kind. Our elders need to take responsibility for our younger ones. But for this to be successful we must be in a place where we are seeking first the Kingdom of God and His righteousness, returning to our first love with no reservations at all.

We have to stand for God's Word, no matter what. We are losing our younger ones because they have not gotten what was needed for their walk. We need to repent and get back to the truth, and so, we can get a grip of those who need our help.

Jesus showed us the Father, and we are required now to show Jesus to others. We are light and salt, and we are called to produce light and be salt as well. People must see Jesus in us and through us. Young Kings must come forth to show forth Jesus the King of Kings and Lord of Lords.

Kings are groomed before conception. Parents must believe and know who they are and know their role. Our heart condition must be in line with God, affirming and declaring who our children and grandchildren are. Speaking into the lives of people who come into our sphere of life, encouraging and training where ever an opportunity is given. Sometimes we have to make an opportunity. In other words we are to make it happen. God will help us if we are determined to see it happen. He gave us the Holy Spirit for this purpose to make things come alive.

As we consider becoming parents preparation for moulding our young kings should begin prayerfully before conception. While these children are in the womb As both parents stay in the presence of God during the pregnancy, washing the embryo with the blood of Jesus, the Holy Spirit will guide the prayers and declarations that should be made over all areas of the child's future. In so doing parents can release the spirit of a Godly mind-set over their children. Parents should also settle within themselves that the priority must not be their will for their children's lives but God's. Consciously dedicating our children to God even while in the womb, can be very beneficial. . Having children now, can no longer be just an ordinary thing. We must have purpose in conception. There is need to be prepared spiritually, releasing from our lives, generational curses and all past hurts and pains so we can go forward without baggage. This is why it is important to encourage our young to keep themselves pure, helping them to understand that their bodies are temples of the living God, and that they are vessels of honour.

The thought- life is so powerful we need to be clean, with pure thoughts because our thoughts will influence their thoughts. We must understand that whatever we do will be influencing the young ones that are being moulded on the inside of us. A king's life is one of sacrifice. Training is necessary, and involves surrendering natural desires. Even though it might look good you cannot do what you feel you want to do because your life is the greatest influence on that king. You are a representative of the Kingdom.

Looking at the babies of this time, I continue to be in awe. They are a special breed. They talk without fear, act like they know everything and they know that they know. They have a power and something that is great inside of them that should be cherished and groomed for such a time as this. I believe this attitude is there to tear the devil's Kingdom down and to spoil his plan totally. These babies must be taught to love and love and love. This love is first geared towards loving God with all that they can understand at an early age. They must be soaked in the spirit of love and the word of Almighty God.

Young kings cannot be groomed without Godly wisdom, understanding, discernment and guidance from the Spirit of God. King Solomon asked God for wisdom. He knew that he could not govern the people without wisdom. We too must understand that we need God's wisdom for this assignment. We have to depend totally upon God to groom His children. There is a certain authority that comes with wisdom. It takes over and takes control with a special anointing to flourish into something beautiful and perfect.

I am seeing some young ones that are very different. Remember young Kings do not mix until they can influence, so they are programmed or trained mostly by the Holy Spirit to be different. Yes they are in the world, but not of the world, and if they go out there it will only be for a while, so we need not worry. All we need to do is what the scripture say. Proverbs 22:6 — "Train up a child in the way he should go, and when he is old he will not depart from it".

They do not fit easily into society, as a matter of fact they have a difficult time, even to the point of getting depressed. They do not find friends easily and if they do, friendships do not last, making them feel something is wrong with them, because everybody else seems happy. The only exception here is if they should find someone like themselves. Parents find it tough to handle such children if they are not guided by the Holy Spirit. They are almost deemed special needs children. These children are specially set aside by God, and He trains them in His way according to what he requires them to fulfil, for the call on their lives. Basic training is necessary for all people to love and obey, honour and glorify God; to give thanks and praise and appreciate what God has done for us and what He has given to us.

The great concern here is that these young ones feel that something is wrong with them, not recognizing that all is well with them. It takes a lot out of parents and those around them to encourage and keep them believing that they are fine.

I believe God releases a special anointing to the parents of these children, like it was with Jesus and John the Baptist. If He did it for them He will do it for us. We must be careful in this end time to consciously and proactively steward the children in our care — these young kings. We cannot take things for granted any more or leave their upbringing to chance.

Almighty God and Loving Father, how we love You and need You more than ever before, we are in dire need of Your Holy Spirit to guide us and help us to groom Your children for this time. A special anointing is necessary, and can only come from You, there is no way that we can do this without You my Lord. We ask this in Jesus Christ's Name.

CHAPTER EIGHTEEN

[A Grandmother's Joy]

As I completed breakfast one morning, I had no idea what special touch of joy would fill this grandmother's heart, when I was sent to a particular street corner to stand. While on these assignments, I learned to be patient, to believe and most of all to be obedient, as the Spirit of God quickens and directs.

As I waited, I would either be praising or praying as the Spirit of God would guide. The directive I received was to stand and wait for someone who would pass by. I looked and waited. Children passed by on their way to school, and I continued to stand. As they did, I saw the different attitudes and behaviour.

As a drizzling rain began, the children gathered under the shop, where I was standing. What I did not know was that the shop was a hang out area until school started. Anything could happen under the shop; what the students could not do or say in school, they could do out there, so some of them waited for school to actually start before leaving.

As I remained there, it got a bit crowded and I could hear some of the conversations. As two of the boys came closer, I heard one of them ask, "Can I get a cigarette?" (a name was added to the request). Then another young guy took out a pack from his pocket and handed it to him. I looked on and I prayed, "Lord what do you want from me?" I knew He allowed this to happen in my presence for a reason, but I was not going to move without guidance. I waited for the quickening inside of me and a peace that I knew to be my Lord's.

I responded as the opportunity presented itself and I was able to get the attention of the young man. With the love of God, I spoke to him as a grandmother. As I spoke to him he bent his head and said to me that his grandmother taught him about God. He had let her down by doing what he knew to be wrong, and he wanted to stop. Even with others around he allowed me to pray for him, and I was able to encourage him to surrender his life to God and be the person God created him to be. God reached out to him that day and reminded him of His Love for him.

When I pray, I am reminded at times to lift up to God all the people with whom God had me come into contact. Not only this young man but others to whom I may have extended God's love through the giving of a book, even a hug or some other form of encouragement. I feel compelled to respond to the quickening of the Holy Spirit when the need arises. I may never see them again or even remember them, but God knows them. As I go, I just thank Him for sending them and giving me the opportunity to be His mouthpiece, and to do His bidding. It is very clear to me now, how the principle of planting seed, watering and increase is established. There are times when I know that I am planting seed, and then when I am watering, but Praise God He gives the increase. You do your part, I do mine and in the fullness of time, we see the results given by God.

Almighty God, You are the Lover of our souls, You created us in Your image and likeness. Father let us as grandparents be Your light, recognizing that we have an opportunity to spread light to the young ones. We may feel that they are not hearing us, but help us to be aware that we must make a difference in their lives, Lord we ask this in the precious Name of Jesus Christ. Amen

CHAPTER NINETEEN

[God's Love Bubbles Over]

On an extremely hot day in the blazing midday sun in the month of September, while preparing to go to town, I felt the urge to walk. I love walking, but being a little tired, I deliberated whether I should walk or take a taxi into Port of Spain. As I stepped out of my gate, I was quickened in my spirit to walk, since I was sure that this was God inspired. Excitement and anticipation captured my very being, and I looked forward to what God was about to do.

As I proceeded I began to feel refreshed and energized, but as I got about a quarter of a mile down the road, I thought, why am I doing this? Reflecting on the fact that I was almost in the city, I started questioning myself, and wondered if I was mistaken. Did I really hear from God? Ahead of me under a closed down liquor store, I noticed a well known homeless man sitting on the curb with his head bent.

Looking on this interesting scene, I noticed this vagrant in his own little world, focused on stripping a cigarette box into small squares. As I passed by, suddenly I heard "He is yours". I was stunned, thinking, He is mine? What am I to do with him? With mixed feelings, a debate started with my Lord.

It is the truth that God created us all in His image and likeness, but (definitely) nothing that I saw in this man looked approachable, and whether or not he mirrored the image and likeness of my God was questionable. Yes! I had to be certain this was God, and if so, this had to be the one occasion that God must have made a mistake. He was a strong, rough looking individual, whose appearance could easily be identified as menacing. Strings were tied around his matted hair which dropped over his face. His gaze was intimidating and you felt that any second he would pounce on you. One could not determine his true skin complexion or the colour of his clothes because of the amount of dirt that covered him. Under all this, who was the real man? People driving past him would turn up their car windows so that they did not have to make contact with him; and even more despicable was his scent that went along with his image, as he approached to ask for cash.

"He is yours" were the words spoken again. Could you imagine? What would you do? Well I kept walking; not as fast as I had been, but nevertheless I kept going at a snail's pace, knowing full well that I needed to turn back in order to please my Lord. I asked "God, what do you mean?! Clearly I heard, "This is the reason for your walking." Still confused at the words, "He is mine" I tried to determine what God really meant by that. Did he belong to me? What should I do? What do I say? My mind continued to process the information, but my spirit was speaking loudly.

A steamy silence followed. Stunned! I said "Okay Lord." I turned around and slowly walked back while I looked at him sitting there in his own world, obviously creating his carpet of beauty with the little squares from the cigarette box. I got very close and he never looked up.

I did not know what to say. I knew I had to say something so as I got right in front of him I opened my mouth and out came "Hello" and I greeted him with the words "Jesus loves you." As the words came out of my mouth there was a great transforming power that beamed into the atmosphere, and immediately I got a vision of that transforming name "JESUS" the name above all names. He looked up at me and I saw the image and likeness of God shining through. His smile was beautiful, his personality gentle, and he answered by telling me about Jesus and His goodness.

As we spoke about Jesus I was amazed to see the love of God bubbling over. He spoke freely, as though a light had been turned on in him, and I realized that that light was the love of the Lord Jesus

Christ flowing out to me. When I thought that God wanted me to minister to this man, he was in a position also to minister to me, which he did. It was such a joy for me as we chatted for a while, feeling God's love all over me, reminding me to never judge a book by its cover.

I knew God through His Holy Spirit, who has taught me quite a lot, was teaching me something new. He was reinforcing how to love the unlovely. It was not about this man and not even about me, but about God's commandment of love and to love His Kingdom's business. Presently as I write I feel God is revealing to me the full implication of this assignment, which I did not quite understand earlier. Impressed upon me is the need to pray this man through until he is off the streets. He may very well be one of God's vessels of honour unto the Lord in this end time season.

"You shall love the Lord your God with all your heart, with all your soul, with all your strength, and with all your mind, and your neighbor as yourself (Luke 10:27)".

We are reminded that God cannot fill the earth with His glory until we are sincerely ready to love as He loves, highlighting our obedience to Him. His glorious presence brings many benefits. As our love for the God of love is released, His Glory will also shine forth, releasing His presence on the earth. I thank the Lord for giving me a glimpse of what can happen as we obey His guidance, although we may not understand, or even when we are faced with a difficult situation. I am fully aware that as we obey the Lord our God and He is glorified, we experience that bubbling over love for Almighty God. I walked away sensing again the excitement and the exhilaration that I felt on the way to town. It was nothing compared to what I had received that afternoon.

Father I thank You for Your love and the mighty gift You have given to us to represent You on this earth. Help us Lord Jesus to see as You see, to hear as You hear, and to feel as You feel so that we can respond to others as You would. We need the ability to be quickened by Your Holy Spirit to fulfill Your plan here, while we await Your return. Help us Lord Jesus! Help! Help!. Amen.

CHAPTER TWENTY

[Becoming Love]

We the people of God become love in Christ Jesus.

There are those people who are born with extra portions of love; those in whose lives God has dealt bountifully. There are others who only achieve this level of love when they experience the love of God Almighty through His Son Jesus Christ, who is love Himself.

I have recognized that only as we love and truly appreciate life and all that surrounds us, a different perspective is placed in our hearts. As our focus changes we see the need to serve others, rather than to be served.

When God created man He created him in His image and likeness which was a perfect image of love. Sin through Adam and Eve caused a tainting and destruction of that love.

Even with that short coming God made a love covenant with Abram now Abraham, which extends to us His children, thereby exhibiting a Father's love.

> God gave us the Law for a time, because Jesus the Law giver was to soon come and fulfill the very essence of the Law, which is love. He would show us the way to live a life of love. Moses' Law therefore was meant to serve as a shadow/forerunner of things to come.

In the beginning God gave Moses the law for His people as a means of having them live in a way to honour Him and each other. Man has never responded well to laws and so he moves from one extreme to the other, either being rebellious or totally regimented.

God gave us the Law for a time, because Jesus the Law giver was to soon come and fulfill the very essence of the Law, which is love. He would show us the way to live a life of love. Moses' Law therefore was meant to serve as a shadow/forerunner of things to come. We are called to adhere to this Law and not to take it lightly. Laws are designed to be obeyed.

"If you love me keep my law and order." "If you love me, k e e p my commandments." John 14: 15.

John the disciple, who wrote this book in remembrance of JESUS, was a great LOVER. He was definitely one of those people who was graced with a greater measure of potential to love. If you look around you will find some of those people. Start looking if you have not seen them yet.

1 Corinthians 13:13 "And now abide faith, hope, love, these three; but the greatest of these is love."

John loved Jesus with his whole being. He did not care what others thought. He made the most of the time he had with Him. In the most intimate fashion he would place his head upon Jesus' breast unconcerned and unaware of other's opinions of this action; so absorbed was he in loving His Lord and receiving His love. This response is specifically what draws us closer to God and He to His people. Jesus was so moved by John's love towards Him that He was able to trust John with the care of His mother, Mary. Each time I think of this, the thought evokes some strange emotions in me, because Mary had other grown children, and yet Jesus left her with John, and He did it in public while nailed to the cross.

John 19:26-27 captures this moment. "When Jesus therefore saw His mother, and the disciple whom He loved standing by, He said to His mother, Woman behold your son! Then He said to the disciple, Behold your mother!" And from that hour that disciple took her to his own home.

Jesus received all of John's love and Jesus honoured him for it. He knew His mother would receive all the love she needed while she grappled with all the pain she would be experiencing as a result of His suffering and death.

One might say 'I was not so blessed to receive this capacity to love at birth, how can I get it?' It is so simple, we do not believe it to be true.
God is Love, His very nature is Love, so He cannot help but Love, He came to earth in the form of man, as the son of man whom we know as Jesus, to suffer and die to save us so that we could return to our former likeness which is LOVE.

"My song is Love unknown
"My Saviour's love for me.
Love to the loveless shown, that they might lovely be
Oh who am I that for my sake,
My Lord should take frail flesh and die?"
(Samuel Crossman 1624-1683)

You must understand, we were made in His image and likeness. Sin messed us up and we became like dirty silver; so tarnished that we could no longer discern our Lord and His ways anymore. We could no longer hear His voice. In this state, the devil was able to become our guide and our leader. God did not intend for this to happen at all, but He allowed man to decide and man decided and fell short and had no way to return to God on his own. The devil thought he had won, but he was mistaken. For GOD's plan went into full force and He took action. His dear Son in agreement came to earth, suffered and died, shed His precious blood for US ALL, that whoever chooses would have eternal life. John 3: 16 says it all. This love is free. God extends it to ALL. "For God so loved the world that He gave His only begotten Son, that whoever believes in Him should not perish but have everlasting life."

As we decide to accept Jesus and what He did for us, heaven takes notice. God all knowing as He is, is fully aware of our decision and guides the Holy Spirit to turn on our love/light-switch. At the point of our decision, God sees us in His image and likeness but we have a responsibility to keep that relationship with Him alive. We must read, study His word, pray, seek His face and assemble with the saints to learn more of Him. Here we become family and learn to love Him and to love one another as He intended.

Expressing love, one to the other can be one of the most difficult tests you will ever face. However, once we submit to our Lord and Master, we will learn, despite the 'unlovely' in each other. Then we begin to experience the fullness of life as we allow Perfect Love to flow through us. As we submit to the will of the Lover of our souls, we become LOVE — AGAPE, and we demonstrate the God kind of love, and not the earthly, selfish, human kind of love that we are taught by the world.

> *1Cor. 13: 4-8 (Amplified Version). "Love endures long and is patient and kind; love never is envious nor boils over with jealousy, is not boastful or vainglorious, does not display i self haughtily.*
> *It is not conceited (arrogant and inflated with pride); it is not rude (unmannerly) and does not act unbecomingly. Love (God›s love in us) does not insist on its own rights or its own way, for it is not self-seeking; it is not touchy or fretful or resentful; it takes no account of the evil done to it [it pays no attention to a suffered wrong].*
> *It does not rejoice at injustice and unrighteousness, but rejoices when right and truth prevail.*
> *Love bears up under anything and everything that comes, is ever ready to believe the best of every person, its hopes are fadeless under all circumstances, and it endures everything [without weakening].*
> *Love never fails [never fades out or becomes obsolete or comes to an end]. As for prophecy (the gift of interpreting the divine will and purpose), it will be fulfilled and pass away; as for tongues, they will be destroyed and cease; as for knowledge, it will pass away" [it will lose its value and be superseded by truth].*

It is evident then, that in Christ we become LOVE and as we grow in love, we love not because we are afraid to break the law but because we are motivated by a deep desire to honour and please the One who has reduced us to love. Our relationship with others begins to flourish as we become so connected to each other that love flows divinely.

Matthew 5:17. "Do not think that I came to destroy the Law or the

Prophets. I did not come to destroy but to fulfill".
A relationship built on love demonstrates the fruit of deep founded happiness and divine strength.

With love, lots of things change. Tension and stress must diminish, and finally be gone, and there is freedom in dealing with each other. When circumstances arrive where we have to correct children or adults, we can do it in love. We are free to be ourselves, letting the truth reign in us. Encouragement will then be one of our watch words. The value of love is so great, it cannot be measured on a scale, because there is nothing that can be used as a balance. In order to experience the full benefit of Love, it must be nurtured. Love really comes in a package for when we become a new creature exhibiting God's love, other things would follow. In an earlier paragraph, I spoke about the Holy Spirit putting on the switch when we make our decision to accept and follow Jesus Christ as Lord and Saviour. The Holy Spirit now becomes part of us as the switch goes on and He too, like Jesus and the Father, is Love, strengthening the fruit of His Spirit to show forth God's Glory.

Galatians 5:22-23 reads. "But the fruit of the Spirit is love, joy, peace, longsuffering, kindness, goodness, faithfulness, gentleness, self-control". If we truly love God, these fruit will be exhibited as we grow and mature in Christ Jesus but it is impossible to exhibit the fruit of the spirit without LOVE (AGAPE).

Jesus came to portray LOVE in all its glory and that He did in a big way. He has left us to carry on what He started. In the beginning God created the world in and with LOVE. He created us in LOVE, to love worship and serve HIM and HIM only. This love is what is going to really make the world turn around. Darkness and selfishness cannot live in the midst of AGAPE [love]. We need to think seriously about the state of the world right now and let the two commandments that Jesus left with us be the center of our lives. They summarize all the commandments. "Love the Lord your God with all your heart, soul, mind and strength and your neighbour as yourself." Leviticus 19:18 reads "You shall not take vengeance, nor bear any grudge against the children of your people, but you shall love your neighbor as yourself: I am the LORD."

Hear, O Israel: The LORD our God, the LORD is one.[a] 5 Love the

LORD your God with all your heart and with all your soul and with all your strength. 6 These commandments that I give you today are to be on your hearts. 7 Impress them on your children. Talk about them when you sit at home and when you walk along the road, when you lie down and when you get up. 8 Tie them as symbols on your hands and bind them on your foreheads. 9 Write them on the door frames of your houses and on your gates. Deuteronomy 6:4-9 (NIV)

We see from the very beginning God had the same message, and He sent Jesus down to earth to demonstrate it. We are reminded in this great Book to teach the children how to love. This gift is something that we need to leave them as an inheritance. LOVE, LOVE and LOVE. Sadly we have strayed, but it is not too late to return. We have a large number of believers on this planet to flood the earth with His love, if only we could forget ourselves, leave all inhibitions behind and obey His law of love.

> It gets easier as you continue to practice loving others selflessly with little or no thought of how you might be offended in the process, and offended you will be. You will begin to love as God loves and as you believe that the Holy Spirit will shed abroad the love of God in your heart. To love unconditionally is wonderful and liberating.

We do not need to know people personally to love them. God has been teaching me, that I am just to love. It is a walk. The spirit of God is the greatest teacher. If you desire the lesson He will teach you. I can talk from my experiences. I am not saying that it is always easy, and we will falter, but we must get up and move on. It gets easier as you continue to practice loving others selflessly with little or no thought of how you might be offended in the process, and offended you will be. You will begin to love as God loves and as you believe that, the Holy Spirit will shed abroad the love of God in your heart. To love unconditionally is wonderful and liberating.

1 John 4:8 "He who does not love does not know God, for God is Love.

Revelation 2:4 "Nevertheless I have this against you, that you have left your first love." The consequences of leaving our first Love reflected in Vs. 5 of this scripture seem exceedingly harsh, but it is true because God said it. "Remember therefore from where you have fallen; repent and do the first works, or else I will come to you quickly and remove your lamp stand from its place-unless you repent." Lord Jesus calls us to repent and return to our first Love. The price that was paid for us is still operating and the powerful blood of the LAMB is still flowing to cleanse us to fulfill our LOVE walk with JESUS. JESUS' love and blood covers our sin. LOVE truly is a heart condition, given to us by His Grace. Receive it and be blessed in JESUS.

LOVE grows and love spreads. If we purpose in our hearts to receive and share this Love, it will spread rapidly. God is waiting on His love birds to fly and once we do He will cause His angels of love to spread His spirit of love even further than we could ever ask or think.

Father in the name of Jesus, I pray that even as this is written, Your Spirit of love will be released and as we read the contents there will be a full blown move of Your Holy Spirit upon us, releasing Your Spirit of Love, love and more love. (Agape). Thank You Father in Jesus' Name. Amen.

CHAPTER TWENTY-ONE

[Sharing God's Love]

I have learned over the years, the importance of seeking God in the early morning as a priority for growth in my spiritual life. It certainly sets the pace for the day. In the quiet of the day, it is so much easier to commune with God and to be able to meditate in His presence, on His word, and to hear His voice. There are times when there seems to be no response, but it is still very refreshing and enlightening to even just sit believing that you are there in His presence. At another time it is just to love on Him and to feel His love flowing all over you. Jesus left us this example in Mark 1 v. 35, where He communed with His Father early in the morning.

It can be difficult at times, even sacrificial, but there are great benefits if we get past all the obstacles. It has surely been a blessing to me. I get most of my guidance and direction at this time, and I feel more equipped to face the day.

As a result, I try to encourage myself and train those around me to do the same, so in my household, once you are trainable this is our practice. My Mum did not do it with me, but this was her approach to the beginning of her day as well. My Mum never woke me, but she got up early and was in God's presence, reading her Bible and praying every morning.

In the earlier days of my sons lives, we worshipped together before they left for school, in this particular scenario it is my three spiritual daughters and I that would have devotions each day before going to school. On Saturday mornings however, we would spend more time discussing the Word of God and relating it to everyday life. This practical application of the scriptures was of great help to me, and I wanted them to be equipped for their journey in life. As we connect the Scriptures to living, so that its reality can be seen and experienced by those around us, the benefits of living a righteous life are highlighted.

For me this was just any ordinary Saturday, but as we completed our worship I got walking orders. I was led to prepare for a trip to the Queen's Park Savannah, which was about fifteen to twenty minutes from my home in Trinidad and Tobago. The Savannah is a popular place where people go to exercise, (walk, run, cycle) or simply relax. You can also purchase lots of special food items such as coconut water, boil or roast corn, etc.

My daughters Isha, Ebony and Trisha like good soldiers were always excited and ready to go when we received directions from God. Before long we were on our way. While walking we sang, prayed, and talked. We were enjoying each other's company as we proceeded, not knowing why we were going or who we would meet. On approaching the side where the Savannah is opposite the Botanical Gardens, I felt led to go to the Botanical Gardens. While walking around the Gardens I saw a lady a little distance away coming towards us. She had a young girl with her and I was encouraged in my spirit to ask her if I could pray with her. I know it sounds strange - how do I know what her prayer needs are?

However, I did ask her, and I hugged her before we began praying. After we were finished praying she told me that her husband was very ill, and things did not look very good. I enquired of her about his relationship with Jesus, and whether he had accepted Him as Lord and Saviour. She said yes. At that point, an older daughter who was also in the Gardens joined us and we agreed that we should all pray together for the situation. We began the second prayer.

I had no idea who this lady was, (she did look familiar) until she told me who her husband was-- a well known and loved Calypsonian for many years.

What a joy it was to know that God had given us this opportunity to share His love and to encourage this family in their time of need. They saw the goodness of God highlighted in His manifested love throughout this situation, reminding them that they were special and mattered to Almighty God.

As the Mum and I chatted, so did the children. I learned then that God did orchestrate this time, preparing both sides to come together in spirit and in truth, by leading us into Praise and Worship as we were on our way to the Gardens, and while they too were walking around the Gardens. God through His Holy Spirit was teaching us of His mighty love, by showing us that we are one family and in need of each other. Another important lesson learned was that we do not have to know who someone is to support them in time of need. We only introduced ourselves after we were finished praying. It never entered my mind before to check to see if it was someone that I knew. I only focused on what I was directed to do. We blessed each other, as we encouraged each other to stay connected to God and to believe God's word. We hugged each other, the children followed suit, and we were on our way.

Father, help us to be so united to You in love, that we will be quickened by Your Holy Spirit, ready to help in time of need, Show us dear Lord the importance of being Your Body of Christ, and how You require us to be so knit together that we forget ourselves and unite in God's love always. Give us a clear vision of Your joining us together in one, in Jesus Name we pray. Amen.

CHAPTER TWENTY-TWO

[God's Peace in Worship]

To my great surprise when I thought the mission we, (my girls and I) were on was completed and we could be about our own business, I was guided by the Holy Spirit to go to one of our hotels around the area to visit a friend who worked there. I did not know if she was on duty but I obeyed and we were on our way. As we started off, down came the rain and there really was no place to shelter in that area, so we happily enjoyed our rain bath.

We got to the hotel and while we were not dripping wet, we were soaked. I felt it was not the best idea to go into the building with wet clothes. Deciding to stay outside, I had to get someone's attention to inquire about my friend.

Unexpectedly, the door opened rather quickly and a gentleman was holding the door wide open for us to enter, I told him that we were not coming in but asked if he could help by finding out if my friend Peggy was at work. He was happy to do so and came back to say that she was not there. Since this was not my first experience of this kind, I smiled to myself knowing that this was a divine set up by God, so I waited intently to see what the next move would be.

The rain continued to fall and the gentleman went back inside and returned after a little while. We stood outside and just talked. As we spoke, we began talking about God and some interesting experiences like the one earlier that day in the Botanical Gardens. We got excited about the things that God was doing, and we inquired as to each other's place of worship. Quickly he shared his place of worship and I responded, "Great". Then suddenly he started sobbing. Well! I was lost, and thought 'Jannetta what did you say wrong'?! I wondered as the girls and I exchanged glances.

After a short period he said to me, "You are the first person that I told where I worship who did not say to me you need to move from where you are; you do not belong there." I was truly lost for words because it never occurred to me to respond negatively to his place of worship. I felt I would have been out of place to do so.

I told him how happy I was to chat with him and to hear what God was doing in his life and encouraged him to continue seeking the Lord and staying in His presence, where he would always know God's will.

I truly felt very happy for him and there was a connection made in the spirit. This was such a powerful experience as I saw God's love exhibited so beautifully by walking in obedience to Him. He surely meets us at our point of need!

God who is aware of our needs, and knows what He wants to achieve to encourage us in our spiritual walk, allowed my brother to fill in on a job assignment which was not his line of work. He was assisting for someone who did not turn up for work that day.

We both laughed, realizing that this was God's divine appointment to bless him by showing him that he does not need to be in a particular place to be a true worshipper or to have a spirit of worship. This brother was in bondage and needed to be set free to worship. As we were preparing to say our goodbyes, we were all very happy and rejoicing at all that occurred, I then felt led and offered to pray for him. We prayed, and then said our goodbyes, hugging and wishing each other well as we went on our way.

Meanwhile, the rain's mission was completed, and so was ours. The sun shone forth in all its glory, and we continued to enjoy the rest of the afternoon, as we dried in the sunlight. Praise be to God!

I can see God's wisdom when He says in the scripture – "In everything give thanks; for this is the will of God in Christ Jesus for you. 1

Thessalonians 5:18." "Giving thanks always for all things to God the Father in the name of our Lord Jesus Christ. Ephesians 5: 20."

I give God praise and thanks that He kept us from grumbling. My girls Isha, Ebony and Trisha were very young. They took these things all in good stead and rejoiced in the Lord always. They are surely good soldiers for the army of the Lord. I know that these experiences would not be wasted and would enhance their walk with God.

I can see as I grow in the Lord that true worship cannot be accomplished until we are walking in obedience to our God. This is why it is so difficult to become a true worshipper. Worship is a life style of obedience and we need to continually strive for this as we serve God. There is such peace when I walk in obedience to God and His Word. There is no comparison to this peace which surpasses all understanding.

Thank You Father for this lesson on worship. Help us dear Lord to understand the importance of obedience and our love for You as we worship You in spirit and in truth, so that we can have that peace, that is beyond our understanding. We ask this in Jesus' Almighty Name. Amen.

CHAPTER TWENTY-THREE

[The Touch of a Father]

I once met a remarkable man, who was exceedingly knowledgeable of the things of this world. He was well spoken, and could answer most questions. Exceptional in many areas of life, yet he was lacking.

Oh yes! What a complex man he was, well endowed financially but a sad man, with a depressed, lonely, and frustrated outlook most times. He had lots of friends and he was in a position of authority, so he could get anything, go anywhere and do whatever he chose. Yet he was a man who did not know God, could not touch God and felt he did not need God, so he did it his way.

Then I met another man. People would describe him as simple. He knew some things, could afford to go to few places, and was able to answer lots of questions.

Always cheerful---He was admired greatly for the joy and peace he exhibited; a peace that caused people to gravitate towards him. Yet there were questions, and people wondered how could he be so happy? Why was he always so cheerful? He was not rich; he had teenagers like many other men. How could he be so calm?

This simple man that I met was like a flag flying high, flowing in the Grace of His God and dancing to the tunes of His Father. So as he went, he knew where he was going and when he spoke he knew what he was saying, and his actions exhibited the very will of Almighty God. He declared Jesus Christ the Lord of his life.

His family knew him as the high-priest. He lived the life of a son of God and he encouraged his beautiful wife to do the same. He taught her well by example, was a great testimony when they courted, and she came into agreement with him, honoured and respected him as a woman of virtue should. When they got married, their life together had so much worth added to it, all because of the decision that they made to allow Jesus to be the Head of their lives and their home. This man surely was the high-priest and trained up his children in the fear and admonition of God.

It became pretty easy for him to handle his teenagers since he taught them to love the Lord and they saw by example, parents who loved the Lord and were obedient to God's Word.

One day the daughter told her parents that she wanted them to meet a friend, a girl she met in class (let's call her Joy). She found Joy to be a nice girl. While Joy was a bit grumpy at times, they talked and she felt that God wanted to do something in Joy's life. Her parents agreed to meet Joy, so she invited her over. Joy's father turned out to be that complicated, sad man that I first met.

Poor child, she was struggling with all that she learnt from her dad, but inside of her was a different person. Joy loved her friend's family and realized that this is what she wanted for her own family. They asked Joy's parents to allow her to go to church with them.

Eventually, after a series of visits, Joy accepted Jesus Christ as Lord of her life and was determined to change her old ways so that she could truly live for Him. She allowed the Word of God to renew her mind, while the Spirit of God drew her closer and closer to Jesus, making it a delight to submit her life to God. The blood of Jesus cleansed and purified her as she continually walked in God's presence.

The Holy Spirit did a great work with her and in her. As a result, her father and mother saw the change and the peace that overtook her. As they observed they each silently yearned to experience the same, yet they did not share their thoughts with each other.

As Joy and her friend became closer, her friend's parents made a commitment to pray for Joy's family as well. Later on they invited them over to a meal, so they could get better acquainted.

One day there was a visiting minister to their church so they invited Joy's parents who eagerly accepted the invitation; one for which, it appeared, they had been silently hoping. They were very excited. Their waiting was over.

As the minister started bringing the message, Joy's father began weeping uncontrollably. He wept almost to the end, while his wife was overwhelmed with what she was hearing. Without a word to each other, even before an altar call was made, they simultaneously made their way quickly to the altar to give their lives over to Jesus. Later on they reflected on the fact that it was the most important decision of their lives.

Joy was the eldest child; she had two very young siblings, a sister and a brother and now with the change in their parents, for the first time, they found themselves in a truly privileged position. Their parents were now in a position to bring them up in the fear and admonition of the Lord Jesus Christ.

From that day of transformation, their father went home a different man with a determination to have this peace that he felt coming from the man of God (Joy's friend's father). He needed this type of family-life and decided to allow God to be the Head of his family.

He studied the Word of God, and strove to become the son, God created him to be. He started praying and reading the Word with his family, and they would praise and worship together. Not only did he study, but he invited his daughter's friend's family to join him as they encouraged each other to love the Lord with all their soul, mind and strength as they would praise and worship together. The two families would gather together at times to exalt the name of JESUS with thanksgiving.

Joy's father became another great light in the community and before long, people, seeing the change in his life, and especially moved by the humility that now characterized him, joined the study of the Word. Soon flags were flying all over this community because of the touch of one Father.

What you have just read is a composite of two different types of fathers one can find in the world.

Will you be that father who comes to his senses, humbles himself and in love and obedience, submits to the Lordship of Jesus Christ?

Father, in this time where we are seeing a decline in fatherhood, we pray dear Lord that Your Holy Spirit would rest upon fathers all over the world. Renew the minds of men on a whole my Lord, helping them to understand who they are and teach them how to be mighty men of God. Wrestle with them Father, that they would return to their calling as Godly fathers, so that they would take up full responsibility at this time. We destroy the yokes and strongholds that have kept them in bondage over the years, and we release them now dear Lord to operate in Your perfect will. Let Your Kingdom come and Your will be done in their lives. Lord we are thankful for those fathers who have stood up, also those who are trying to do their best. We bless them and all fathers in the mighty Name of Jesus Christ. Amen.

CHAPTER TWENTY-FOUR

[A Father's Legacy to His Son]

What have you inherited? What is the legacy that you are leaving for your children?

God described King David as "A man after God's own heart". Everything that he did in his life was as a result of his passion for His God, including how he chose to respond when he sinned. He honoured the Word of God in all ways. Yes he did sin, but he never failed to acknowledge his wrong, truly repent and move on.
King David not only left a priceless legacy for his son Solomon, but his example benefits us profoundly up to this day. As we look at his life we will see countless lessons that can help us to live a better Christian life.

There is no greater teaching than for a child to see his father, (or mother if the father is absent) live out the Word of God.

King Saul disobeyed God and yet King David, because of his love for Father God, honoured him. 1 Samuel 13:1-15 records King Saul's unlawful sacrifice. Samuel had to make a sacrifice unto the Lord and when King Saul saw that he was late, he decided to offer the sacrifice himself. Verses 13 and 14 read, 'And Samuel said to Saul "You have done foolishly. You have not kept the commandment of the Lord your God, which He commanded you. For now the Lord would have established your Kingdom over Israel forever. But now your Kingdom shall not continue. The Lord has sought for Himself a man after His own heart, and the Lord has commanded him to be commander over His people, because you have not kept what the Lord commanded you." Even though God responded this way, David stayed on course with God's Word. David loved the Lord and wanted to obey His word. David not only honored King Saul, but we see later on, that he honoured his children and grandchildren also.

David made a statement in the way he responded to the men who thought they were coming to bring good news to David when Saul was killed. They hurried to bring the news joyfully, but David made it clear that he would not be a part of their actions. As a result lives were lost. A great lesson for us to remember; we should never be a part of what is against the Word of God. This must be obvious in our lives for our descendants to observe, to help them make right decisions when that time comes.

Gossip, slander, fault finding and lots of other little shady areas that do not seem to amount to much, can cause serious problems and destroy not only our lives, but also leave a poor legacy for our children, even as far as causing generational curses. It is important for us to turn to things that are Godly so that our children will have examples and inherit blessings instead of curses from us. Fathers, mothers, grandparents are all responsible for living righteous lives in order to pass on Godly legacies to their children.

If our children see us praying through trials and tests, standing upon God's Word, and even including them as part of the prayer team they would learn and develop the same practice. However, on the other hand, if we respond in a manner that declares there is no hope, and we are not looking to Jesus as our hope, that response is exactly what they will learn. As we respond to situations in the flesh, which reflects how we feel, and think, in other words flesh shows up as strong, then this is really what we are teaching those around us .

Do you swear when something happens? Then what do you expect to happen with your child? Can you imagine living in a house with someone who, when a crisis occurs, starts praising God and "Thank you Jesus" comes out of their mouth? If your child sees this more than any other reaction, don't you think that reaction is what they will be inclined to imitate more than anything else? You may be hurt and cry, but still put God in His place of prominence.

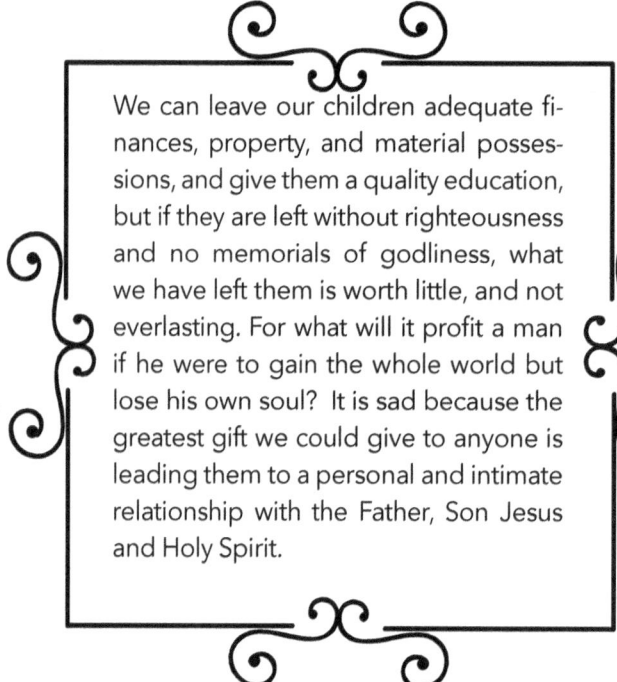

We can leave our children adequate finances, property, and material possessions, and give them a quality education, but if they are left without righteousness and no memorials of godliness, what we have left them is worth little, and not everlasting. For what will it profit a man if he were to gain the whole world but lose his own soul? It is sad because the greatest gift we could give to anyone is leading them to a personal and intimate relationship with the Father, Son Jesus and Holy Spirit. Many people quote from the Bible about fathers leaving an inheritance for their children, but with limitations because it is only worldly inheritance. This needs to be rectified. God is always first.

The Lord spoke to Joshua and told him that he must build a memorial for the children of Israel forever ---Joshua 4:1-7. Joshua summoned 12 men, one from each tribe, to get a stone each from the Jordan over which they had recently crossed despite all odds. They were to build a memorial so that when their children saw it and asked they would tell them what the Lord had done. This is their legacy. Memorials are part of legacy, and they are tangible to our heart and mind. Teaching our children to love the Lord is our greatest legacy.

1 Chronicles 28 records King David in exhortation to the people. This to me is mind blowing, even though he was a man after God's heart, as a bloody man of war, King David could not build the Lord's

House and Courts. Yet the Lord gave him the pattern as an inheritance for his son Solomon who was to follow as king. An inheritance is whatever is passed on, be it good or bad, valuable or invaluable.

Verse 8, "Now therefore, in the sight of all Israel, the assembly of the Lord, and in the hearing of our God, be careful to seek out all the commandments of the Lord your God, that you may possess this good land, and leave it as an inheritance for your children after you forever." We are therefore expected to leave an inheritance or legacy for the next generation to be able to build on, so that they can move to another level. The king went on in Ch. 29:2 to say, "Now for the house of my God I have prepared with all my might," so he adds a challenge by telling them all that he was leaving to help build his Lord's house. This stirred up the people to meet the challenge that King David extended to aid them in their offering to the building of the Lord's house.

Who would have a heart not to respond when the example that the King had set was so great, and was done wholeheartedly to their God. Commitment was made of gifts and service and reference was made to a perfect heart in offering. They offered willingly and with a glad heart. This resulted as worship to the LORD. He was highly exalted over all, and the King and the people rejoiced gladly before Him. An inheritance or legacy can be seen in many different ways. A right attitude plays an important part in our day to day lives and is therefore inherent in our legacy. This is so very important as we serve and communicate with each other in all areas of leadership. Daniel left a legacy - his worship and honour to God.

His entire life style caused a whole nation to turn towards GOD. His detractors thought they knew how to destroy him, yet he persevered in praying as he kept his commitment to worship God. There was no compromise as far as Daniel was concerned. He never changed his position in prayer or cut back on his time with God, even when he knew that they were after him. He was sure that he was following a Holy God and he was determined to live a holy life that would be acceptable unto God. They sought ways to bring him down, yet they could not.

Jesus' inheritance to us is unblemished. While on earth, He lived a life of Holiness, showing us that we too can do the same. We have a guarantee in Christ Jesus, and a helper in the Holy Spirit. He is the

way, the truth and the life, so if we follow His example and live our lives by God's Word, our lives would be a guaranteed legacy.
Recently, one of my sons and a few of us were discussing travelling stand by. Have you ever travelled stand by? There is an uncertainty experienced not knowing for sure when or if you will be afforded a seat. This can cause a feeling of anxiousness, especially when the passenger list is long.

Comparing this scenario to the Kingdom, it is so beautiful to know that we all have an equal chance for a seat. We can be seated in heavenly places if we take the right course of action. In standby, seats are determined according to rank, years of service etc. In this arena, one can make adequate provision, yet there is no guarantee, because you have no control. It depends on who decides to travel on the day you travel. With Kingdom business, once you have made provision by accepting Jesus Christ as Lord and Saviour you are guaranteed a seat, and this is a major part of our child's inheritance. This extends not only to our children, but is a Godly legacy for those who God has placed around us to nurture by example, or teach in some form. Our legacy from the early church has been great. Are we going to let it go to waste?

So, fathers and mothers, elders, what legacy are we leaving for our children??? Are we prepared to make a sacrifice to leave a Godly legacy for our loved ones to make sure they are secured in Christ Jesus, and are going to inherit that place Jesus went to prepare for us? Just like it is the most beautiful gift God gave to us when He gave us His one and only Son to die on the cross and rise to give us eternal life, so we must leave a Godly legacy if we so love our loved ones.

Father, we are in need of Your help to bring us to a place of reckoning, to see the need to live our lives in such a way that is pleasing in Your sight, helping us to restore the truths we have lost, and helping our generations to benefit by a solid Godly life. It is necessary Lord, so please open our eyes that we may see where we have gone wrong, and have the desire to surrender all to You, to turn things around, so that You may be glorified as the Sons of God arise to worship You in spirit and in truth. Father we ask this in Jesus' mighty Name, the Name that is above all names. Amen.

CHAPTER TWENTY-FIVE

[We Are All Called to Be Teachers]

God's unique, distinguished plan for His church is the perfecting of the saints through His fivefold ministry. He has given us Apostles, Prophets, Evangelists, Pastors and Teachers under His guidance to feed, guide, encourage, correct in love and assist in maturing the flock ensuring that we are ready for the work that HE has set out for us.

Who is a teacher? Our dictionary gives definitions, but for a simple explanation, I would like to say any one who can be seen or heard can and does teach. We learn from each other every single day, and our lives are impacted in so many ways by what we see and hear outside of a formal teaching facility. The first requirement for a teacher is to be "teachable". I do not believe that you can teach if you are not willing to be taught.

The course is set and the plan is perfect, but we must be aware of our purpose and destiny. It is necessary for the Holy Spirit to take total control of all that we do and so lead us into all truth, ensuring that as we fulfill our purpose, God's Glory would be evident. God is ready for HIS Glory- in all it's splendour - to be shown forth all over the earth to destroy the works of the evil one.
1 Peter 5: 2 tells us that God wants His flock fed. How are we to feed the flock? Who is supposed to feed the flock? When should the flock be fed? The saints are the flock, and the Shepherd is responsible for feeding the flock.

As children of God, we are all called to be teachers, true worshippers and disciples. When we accept Jesus Christ as Lord and Saviour, we are automatically grafted in as members of God's family! His children are called to follow in His footsteps and become like Him. As we fellowship with the Father, His Son Jesus and the Holy Spirit and sit in His family under His leadership, we grow into God's likeness. This is where our formal teaching begins. It would be a selfish act, if, as we learn, we keep it to ourselves and not pass it on. Our only qualification here is submission and a teachable spirit. Apostle Paul in Ephesians 4:8-14 gives us a full explanation for why this plan was put in place; we are to be edified and perfected for the Glory of God.

Feeding of the flock happens in many different ways. We all qualify to spread the Good News, to show forth the Light of God and to be salt in the earth.

Feeding and teaching are one and the same. As we are being taught we too are expected to teach. As we grow in the Lord we teach by example, while helping others when necessary. As we love, we are teaching others how to love and we are also spreading the spirit of love into the atmosphere around us. We are called to love as we go, and as we love we will be encouraged and equipped to teach by example.

Jesus as our great Teacher, used many methods of teaching and the Holy Spirit continues the process as He empowers us as Disciples to teach.

God, who is Love, sent His Son Love, to teach us how we are to love in order to establish His kingdom on the earth.

I am convinced that for God's will to be done on earth, we must LOVE as HE LOVES -Love HIM with all our heart, soul, mind and strength and love our neighbour as ourselves. The atmosphere is affected by LOVE. Try it and see what happens. Express love to your plants, animals even your material stuff. This may sound strange, but is it not true that what you love and appreciate and care for lasts longer than something that you do not care for as much? Love is powerful and magnetic, the most precious resource that we have, and is available from our God—LOVE Himself. We are not taught love in a classroom. It is naturally God and God alone.

God created us from love and to love is the reason for our creation. While we are being taught, we too are to teach. As we receive, we are expected to pass it on to others because this helps us to grow and affect the earth in a positive way.

We teach through the word of our testimony. This is a very effective method. The scripture says that we overcome the devil by the blood of the Lamb and the word of our testimony. People are moved by our testimony and we advance the Kingdom and God's work when we testify of His goodness and His grace. We need to let people know that His mercy is new every morning.

The way we respond to trials, tests and encounters speaks loudly about our walk with the Lord. Children of God are always under scrutiny. People are watching us when we are not aware that they are, and they know how we should respond, especially under pressure. Rightfully so, we are to show forth God's grace, since He said His grace is sufficient for us in time of need. We are never really lacking, once we are hooked into our Lord and Saviour Jesus Christ. Even before people are conscious of the need of a Saviour, they are to be taught or fed. Sometimes they do not even know that they are in need of a meal.

Saul was the keeper of cloaks while Stephen was being stoned. He stood and looked on, but Saul never knew he was receiving a meal while he stood there. His spirit was fed by Stephen's words, and these words were stored in his mind. God's plan was to use this testimony as Stephen spoke about His Lord to replay these words in Saul's mind. Saul must have heard these words repeatedly. God used this testimony to bring Saul into his destiny.

Sometimes we get frustrated when people do not seem to hear what we are saying, but we really do not need to worry. We just have to do what we are called to do and leave the rest to God. It is God's church and He said, "I will build my Church and the gates of hell will not prevail against it."

We only need to be aware that as God's children He is in need of us to do what needs to be done. As His family, we are the ones to teach others about Him. This call is full time. We are never on vacation once enlisted. The truth must always prevail. The name of Jesus must be exalted whether we are at home, work or socializing. It is absolutely necessary for the light switch to be on at all times so the light can pierce the darkness no matter what the circumstances.

I can attest from my own experience, that there were times I never knew I was under scrutiny until someone mentioned the occurrence and how my response impacted the person involved, sometimes good or bad. I thank God for keeping me, so that I can be a testimony for Him.

> *Colossians 3: 16 " Let the word of Christ dwell in you richly in all wisdom; teaching and admonishing one another in psalms and hymns and spiritual songs, singing with grace in your hearts to the Lord."*

God has given to us all that we need and has directed us as to how it should be used. We are required to put on charity which is Love and to let the Peace of God rule in our Hearts. Then as we become one in Christ, we are to teach and admonish each other and this will automatically extend to those with whom we come into contact in our everyday lives. We exhibit an especially sweet spirit when we are in tune with God. The Spirit in us then draws people to us, and in this way we become great vessels who help to establish God's Kingdom.

> Tests will come to help us determine where we are in our walk and whether we exhibit light or darkness. At these times, whatever is deep within us will come to the surface, since most people are hardly capable of pretending when under pressure. It is very important to be so filled with the Word and the Spirit that good fruit will be manifested.

Tests will come to help us determine where we are in our walk and whether we exhibit light or darkness. At these times, whatever is deep within us will come to the surface, since most people are hardly capable of pretending when under pressure. It is very important to be so filled with the Word and the Spirit that good fruit will be manifested.

We are called to be transparent, as Jesus was when He walked on the earth.

Lessons could be taught one on one, helping with a specific area or just in general, as a need is met in love. Love must be our watch word. Anything we do that is motivated by anything other than love, will fail. Only Christ through His Spirit can help us to love as God requires. This must be our main focus--- JESUS CHRIST ALWAYS.

The first stage of our performance as teachers is in our homes. This seems to be the hardest place to perform as we should. It is easy to be nice to people for a short while, but for long periods, and with your very own, this is when it becomes a challenge. But if we can get it right in our homes first, by showing forth the love and the Word of God, then we are truly on our way to perfection.

One's greatest impression is made in one's early years of life.

As a Methodist, I was influenced by some of the teachings in the Adventist church through my cousins, who are Adventist. Their father, a Minister, would sometimes preach at a church close to our home, so I would attend with them. They would also visit with us and I with them, so we grew up very close as children. Attending an Adventist secondary school helped me to understand some Biblical principles as well, and this enhanced my walk with God later on in life. One of the lessons that stayed with me was tithing, which I do not remember as being emphasized in my home church.

Many years later when part of my responsibility was fund raising for repairs at my home church, there was an issue, and I was concerned. It caused some tension. While it did not directly involve me, I felt the Lord reminding me about tithing and encouraging me to begin. In response, I started tithing and realized that God allows us to experience things that He uses for the building of His church. Since then I have been faithful in paying tithes and I am very excited when I pay tithes. I have seen God's hand stretched out in my walk, providing in all areas of my life, giving prosperity in my health, and my needs are always met according to His riches in glory. This was a great lesson taught when I was a child. The Spirit of God will always stir up what we learned at the right time, so that it can be used for His Kingdom's sake. We also, always stand to benefit greatly. As a result I use this as a testimony for others about tithing.

I learn by observation, I am more of a practical learner, so I benefit from the right people around me, and I have learned over the years to focus on the mature Christians who are eager to walk with God. I would not follow blindly, but with the Word as my guide, I would quietly look at the examples that God would highlight for me.

We can learn from all peoples. For me there is always something to learn. We just need to have God's wisdom, guidance through His Word and the spirit of discernment to know what to receive and what we are to leave alone.

As teachers, be reminded that we are also students since life is a continuous learning process. Our effort as teachers is reflected long after our earthly life has ended, since those who learn from us continue to teach others. We must therefore be careful to teach what God requires. Through the scriptures we are still learning from what was taught, for instance what Paul taught Timothy and those around him, so many years ago. I thank God that He gave to us His Son Jesus Christ and the precious Holy Spirit who is with us always as our world's greatest Teacher. Let us be excited to teach as Jesus taught.

As we approach this end time season, we have to be more conscious of what our lifestyle and activities are saying to those around us. The line between what is of God and what is right in the eyes of our society can be easily blurred. We must be sure to exhibit Godly principles, integrity and lifestyles of LOVE, so others can clearly see the difference.

If we are off the course that God has called us to be on, it is necessary for us to repent and get back on course, in order to be true examples of His light on the earth. We cannot be that quality of teacher until we turn away completely from our wrong and be in right standing with God, remembering that Jesus warns us of the consequences of causing others to stumble in the Way:

Matthew 18:6-7 "Whoever causes one of these little ones who believe in Me to sin, it would be better for him if a millstone were hung around his neck, and he were drowned in the depth of the sea. Woe to the world because of offences! For offences must come, but woe to that man by whom the offence comes!"

As we teach, we encourage and support each other - the weak are strengthened by the strong. That way we embrace each other and we become links that cannot easily be broken. The evil one is seeking whom he may devour. As we link together in Love, it becomes much more difficult for him to devour. Let us teach by Godly example as exhibited by Jesus the Christ. Remember we are all teaching, but the decision is ours as to what we are teaching.

Abba Father, today I pray that as we read this chapter, all spirits of arrogance and pride, which would prevent us from having teachable spirits and hearts to receive from You Lord would be destroyed right now in the precious name of JESUS CHRIST THE ONE AND ONLY TRUTH. Heavenly Father let JESUS be exalted through our diligence to Your Word in JESUS' Name. Amen.

CHAPTER TWENTY-SIX

[The Footsteps of Your Heart on Land]

I woke up this morning with this song in my heart and on my lips. I just kept singing it repeatedly for a long while. It just would not leave me. This is the song.

> *I wonder what the footsteps of my heart would look like on land.*
> *Holy Spirit take my feet and show my steps.*
> *I just want the world to see My Friend. (This my friend is JESUS CHRIST.)*

It got me thinking, and I realized the Lord wanted something said, so I waited on Him.

Our footsteps represent us - what we do, where we go, how we walk, and even how we talk. We make many steps in our years on the earth. Have you ever thought about the number of steps you make in one year or even one day? What are they about? What do they say? Does it amount to much?

God gave to us dominion over the earth and all things. This land is ours to do with as God expressed. Do we choose to follow God's express will and purpose for the land-- His land? What do I choose? What do you choose? How do we decide what we do with this beautiful land given to us by the Father to tend and to keep? - Then the Lord God took the man and put him in the Garden of Eden to tend and keep it (Genesis 2:15).

We choose whom we would follow. If we are led by the evil one, the negative consequences are limitless, but if we are led by the Spirit of God we are assured of delighting our Lord and agreeing with His perfect will. Psalm 37:23-24 says, "The steps of a righteous man are ordered by the Lord, And He delights in his way. Though he fall, he shall not be utterly cast down. For the Lord upholds him with His hand."

This is great! If only we will allow ourselves to walk in righteousness, then we are led by the Lord and even if we stumble or fall we will be fine because God is in control. If we do not allow our steps to be ordered by God, someone else would surely be ordering them. Let's look at King Solomon the wisest man who ever lived. When he started his reign as King, God was ordering his steps. He was doing well. He followed in his father's steps and God delighted in him. He was blessed in all directions, but 1 Kings 11:2, 4 reads, "From the nations of whom the Lord had said to the children of Israel, You shall not intermarry with them, nor they with you. Surely they will turn away your hearts after their gods." Solomon refused to follow God's command and embraced those very women and clung to them in love. "For it was so, when Solomon was old, that his wives turned his heart after other gods; and his heart was not loyal to the Lord his God, as was the heart of his father David."

What we see here is that Solomon started walking with God and then in disobedience, his walk was taken over by another leader, thinking he could remain in control. Remember he had been the wisest man on earth. But what we do will always catch up with us, if not in our youth, then later in our adult life. Disobedience to God with no repentance leaves a lot to be desired. Solomon was not the only one who paid; so did his children. God in His mercy, even though He decided to tear the kingdom from him, left it until after he died, and still gave his son a part of the benefits; but the rest to his servant.

Many people will walk in and out of your life but only true friends will leave good prints in your heart. Likewise, many thoughts will enter your mind, but only Godly thoughts will leave Godly prints on your heart.

What are our steps saying? Do they go to the little child who may need a meal or a book for school? Do they go to do a parental deed for the motherless or fatherless child?

Are our steps heading in the right direction where God is guiding us to take a word to a destitute, to someone whose son got shot; or a mother dying from cancer and worried about her young ones she is leaving behind? Are we led to a store to buy Bibles to give to someone who accepted Jesus Christ as Lord and cannot afford one? Are your feet prepared to carry the gospel of Peace to the needy?

Are you this person? ... I am in the office and there is a young man who seems to need some advice as to how he treats his wife. Are my steps ready to lift him in prayer and wait on the Lord for further guidance as to what to say to him; or do I decide my feet were made for walking away because that is not my business? So I can easily think, "I know how to treat my wife, he will learn." Or as a man of God with experience and wisdom that can be shared, am I willing to help this young man?

Are the numbers of my steps to the bank so many that the ones to missions cannot be seen? What is recorded in heaven about my footsteps? Is it of any account? Are the soles of my shoes worn out for the Lord? Normal steps on the land are not very easy to see with the normal eye, but if you went through bushes, you would know that someone was there, because the plants would also show signs of being trampled upon. If the weather is bad and there is mud, you would also know, but the normal footprints that do not take much effort are not seen.

Which ones are yours, and which ones are mine? My heart's desire is a record in heaven. I do not care about the one on earth that is of no value when the time comes for accounting. Have my steps been faithful to walking where God has called me to walk? In heaven the steps recorded will not be all the steps that we take, only the ones that have the print of Jesus' blood upon them revealing sacrifices and purposeful love prints. The blood determines the value of the step. The blood shows forth footsteps of God's love. Those are the true footsteps to heaven. We are no longer called to animal sacrifice, but our lives are to be a living sacrifice, one that is alive while we are alive.

At election time, when the votes are counted it is not all the ballot papers that are of value. The rejected, spoilt or destroyed are not counted but the ones upon which the 'x' mark is clear, those are the ones counted. There are even queried ballots if the crossing of the 'x' is above or below the line of the candidates' name. These queried ballots would be like some of our footsteps, which may or may not be rejected. Their value depends upon in whose name they were manifested. Sometimes it may be in the name of Jesus, in whose name it should rightfully be; at other times it is in our own name. Let us use as our help Psalm 17:4-5, "Concerning the works of men, by the word of Your lips, I have kept away from the paths of the destroyer. Uphold my steps in Your paths, that my footsteps may not slip."

Psalm 119:133, "Direct my steps by Your word, And let no iniquity have dominion over me."

God is an excellent God and He wants us to have excellent steps, so if we desire Him and His word and receive Jesus as our Lord and Saviour, He will do it for us, so that when we look at our footsteps we will see the print of our heart, which represents Jesus' heart and His blood. Dedicate our steps to Him and let them be ordered by HIM in LOVE.

Oh Father!! Help us to be Your true representatives. Show us the way Lord and keep our steps ordered by You and You only, so that our footprints will be left for others to use as examples of Your love and life. Let us not falter Almighty God, and if we do convict our hearts so that we will quickly continue in Your perfect will. We ask this in Jesus Christ's precious Name. Amen.

CHAPTER TWENTY-SEVEN

[The Song: Where Would I Have Been?]

Where would I be if not for your grace carrying me in every season
Where would I be if not for your grace, you came to my rescue and
I want to thank you for your Grace. (Repeat)

Grace that restores
Grace that Redeems
Grace that releases me to worship
Grace that repairs visions and dreams
Grace that releases miracles, your Grace
(Repeat Verse)

Vamp:
Grace that restores
Grace that Redeems
Grace that releases me to worship
Grace that repairs visions and dreams
Grace that releases miracles

Grace that repairs visions and dreams
Grace that releases miracles

Grace that restores
Grace that Redeems

Grace that releases miracles

Grace that repairs visions and dreams
Grace that releases miracles
Ending:
Where would I be if not for your grace?
Where would I be? If not for your grace carried in me in every season, where would I be if not for your grace you came to my rescue and I want to thank you, for your grace.
Grace like a river[1].

---

[1] Excerpt from Where Would I Be? – Israel and the New Breed https://www.youtube.com/watch?v=sN2Y99GBYDE

CHAPTER TWENTY-EIGHT

[How Does One Walk With God?]

Jesus is a masterful teacher. In His Word there is example upon example of our Lord using the everyday things of life to reveal the deeper mysteries of the Kingdom of Heaven. One of the most beautiful examples of this is the wilderness tabernacle of the Most High God. The tabernacle was the place ordained by God in which the believer was to be introduced to the Lord, be sanctified and to bear witness of His glory and His might as He abode in His holy presence.

As one takes a virtual tour of the tabernacle from the Gate Beautiful to the most hallowed place - the Holy of Holies, one sees clearly outlined the spiritual journey every believer is invited to take as he or she grows in spiritual maturity and passion for our Lord and Saviour. Allow me to illuminate the critical steps of this journey.

STEP (1)

The believer first enters the tabernacle through His Gate Beautiful. Aptly named because it is the most beautiful thing to see. Someone who was formerly lost, accepts Jesus as Saviour, the One ordained by God to be the Only Way (gate) through which the new believer can gain access to God the Father and benefit from the fullness of joy in His presence.

STEP (2)
Secondly He washes us at the Lavar. Through God's salvation, Jesus' blood is now applied to the believer's soul and he/she be-

comes renewed like a clean, fresh, new born baby in Father God's holy arms.

STEP (3)

Thirdly He heals us and fills us. As we 'enter' the store house of Oil and Wine, He pours His anointing Oil - THE HOLY SPIRIT - upon us and He fills us up with Himself as well. He who is the new wine, makes us new wine skins for Himself; temples for His eternal dwelling.

STEP (4)

Next, HE causes us to proceed to the Store house of Wood. HE knows we are ready for a closer, more personal walk with HIM. Wood is used for many things, especially for building. At this point in the journey, the Lord starts to build HIS character in us. HE does this by applying our old self or previous life to a spiritual Wooden CROSS. Subsequently, this store house leads us directly into another gate where intimacy prevails. Sadly, few make it through this gate.

STEP (5)

Next, comes a most important step in the life of a believer - the entry into the Great Gate. Here is where greatness is accomplished in the realm of the spirit. This is the place where Sons of God take on the image of JESUS the beloved SON OF THE FATHER. I call it the grooming stage. Here you are becoming more and more ATTACHED to HIM; a LEVITE, and worshipper in the true sense.

STEP (6)

Proceeding from the Great Gate, the Lord Jesus directs His new son to the Court of the Israelites. He is your King and God and you are His Isaac; a living sacrifice unto Him. In this court you are called to willingly lay down your life for Him. He carries you to His Slaughter Place, then to His altar of Sacrifice. These two places are symbols of death to self, the old way of living and to wrong thinking and acting, making the way clear to live according to God's way of thinking and doing. In other words, HIS kingdom is allowed free reign in your life and His will is done in you as it is in heaven.

The Altar has steps all the way around. One side faces the Great

Gate, and the other side faces the entry to the Holy Place. On this altar, we could choose to stay and God works in our lives, then to be carried into HIS private space called the Holy Place, or we could jump off the Altar of Sacrifice and head back through the Great Gate and then through the Beautiful Gate, back into our old lives. This is called BACKSLIDING. Many take this way out to their own demise and destruction when the Christian life becomes too hard; when there is too much of this world to be given up. You could jump off this altar at any time.

STEP (7)

If you do not Backslide, HEAVENLY BLISS AWAITS YOU FROM HERE ON. Here we are swept up like a bridegroom sweeps up his beloved and carries her over the threshold of their new home. God carries HIS CHILD/SERVANT/BRIDE into the Holy Place; a place where there is feasting and where HIS LOVE lights up the room. Together you eat of HIS BREAD of LIFE, and drink of HIS wine. Here He soothes you and restores you. Here you have a level of friendship and intimacy with the Lord you never had before. From this place the statement you make to the world is I am forever attached to my God and FATHER, and the Lord JESUS.

STEP (8)

Finally you arrive at the HOLY of HOLIES; the pinnacle of intimacy. After feasting and abiding in the light of HIS love, God carries HIS BRIDE into the Chamber of HIS Passion. Here we hear the words of love echoed, I AM MY BELOVED AND HE IS MINE, as well as TWO HAVE BECOME ONE. Finally God has found HIS true mate. The words, "it is not good for man to be alone" have been replaced by the words, "SPIRIT OF MY OWN SPIRIT AND BONE OF MY OWN BONE". Angels are rejoicing and all of earth has stopped groaning for the sons of God have been manifested. All tears are wiped away and all things have become new. NO TURNING BACK, FROM HERE ON WE WILL LIVE IN "NOTHING MISSING NOTHING LACKING", HALLELUJAH AND SHALOM.

Author's Acknowledgements

My Abba Father God, Lord and Saviour Jesus Christ, Precious Holy Spirit, for You, no assignment You give to me would be left incomplete, no matter the cost. My love for You is too great not to run at Your bidding. Thank You for working in me the power to will and to do of Your good pleasure (Philippians 2:13).

My mother, Gladys Isadora Collins and my father, "Robert" Peter Isaac Collins exhibited God's love in caring not only for their children but anyone else who needed help. They opened up their doors at a moment's notice, paving the way with much generousity of spirit and discipline, for me to carry on their legacy of giving and sharing.

My siblings Alma, Mano, Walter, Joan, Winfield and Lewis served as early role models and encouragers for me in many different forms.

A special thanks to my Sons Nikita, Vivian, Ilya, Lyle and Godfrey, their wives and my many grandchildren for always supporting my decisions even though they may not have fully understood what I was doing when I would open up our humble home to share our little with so many. This greatly impacted their role as fathers. Thanks much for your love always. I could not have reached this far without you all.

I thank God for all those who saw me through this Throne Room assignment providing prayer support, editing, proofreading, design, and publishing. Without this sacrifice of love, I would never have made it.

Godfrey and Natalie, Noelle and Ethan Mark, for their cherished love, support and planning.

Heartfelt thanks to Trinidad Christian Center; Apostle Austin John de Bourg, my Pastor Kelvin Siewdass, and all ministerial staff who motivated me to actively pursue intimacy with the Lord, to do my part in restoring truth that the enemy has stolen from the church, to lay self down for the benefit of another, and to grow in unwavering faith. My precious sisters, brothers and "children" who have poured out much love, prayer and encouragement, including Althea Bastien, Sandra Fabien, Troy and Charlene Pollonais, Wayne and Glenis Vincent, and Cecil and Colleen Davis, Reverends William and Margaret Seedansingh and the visitation ministry family.

I honour Rev. William Watty, Rev. Mural, Rev. Clarke, Reverend Elaine Joseph (Twinnie), Reverend Franklyn Manners, Margaret Alexander, Merle Hoyte, Ms Patrick, Bernice James, Sylvia Sucre, Ida Berry, Louise Ramsden, Deborah Quashie, Polynetta Maxime and the prayer group of the Methodist Church in Trinidad, Pastor Daniel and Glendine Rosales of the Divine Reconciliation International Ministries.

Colleen Davis, my right hand in this entire project who exhibits all of the fruits of a Proverbs 31 woman in the making, staying side by side while, her beloved husband Cecil supported behind the scene. Thanks much.

Richard and Frances Patterson who opened up their home in North Carolina where much of the book was birthed. Reverends Frederick and Annette Coombs, their daughter Karlene, Kenny and Lovern Ryce and Allison Ryce for their support, prayer and inspiration. Audrey Mc Dowall, Sandra Fabien, Evelyn Samm, Sarah Reid, Debra Coleman and Reverend Joe Ella Darby, for their willingness to edit. Sometimes their feedback felt like sand paper, but it was worth it.

Mark Hernandez, a man of valour and Publisher extraordinaire; Ryan Drye, graphic designer, who displayed the love of God through his extraordinary generousity to a stranger.

My Greenforest Community Baptist Church family - Reverend Dennis Mitchell (former Pastor), who so kindly offered to write the Foreword. Minister Rhonda Hicks, Fulfillment Hour class leader, Minister Jeanette Cody, former leader of the evangelism team, Sister Sarah Reid former leader of the prayer group, and sisters and brothers for lovingly embracing me on my arrival in Georgia.

My dear nephew and Author, Kevin Collins, nieces Joanne Edwards, Jacintha Edmund and Jonelle Porter, thank you so much for all your love and support. I especially acknowledge Jacintha (Author) for her faithfulness and obedience to the guidance of the Holy Spirit to deliver the contents of the last chapter "How does One Walk with God?" to me.

Last but certainly not least I honour my 'Jonathan', Elder Margaret 'Peggy' Ng-See-Quan of the Church of Scotland, a champion in her own right.

—Jannetta Collins-Johnson

[Prayer]

Thank You my Lord for the privilege to be used as Your vessel to bring forth this message. I pray oh Father that Your Spirit of Truth, Love, Peace, and Obedience would rest upon us, work through us and bring us to the place where You desire us to be at this time to show forth the true reflection of You JESUS CHRIST. LORD JESUS I ask You to reveal Yourself to us in a mighty way, so that there is no doubt that You are the only way, the One True and Living God. Please Lord let Your Kingdom come and Your will be done. In Jesus' Almighty Name Amen.

Jannetta Collins-Johnson, Author

www.ingramcontent.com/pod-product-compliance
Lightning Source LLC
LaVergne TN
LVHW061214060426
835507LV00016B/1922